WILD HIGHLANDS

WILD
HIGHLANDS

L. MacNally

ILLUSTRATED WITH 74 PHOTOGRAPHS
BY THE AUTHOR

J. M. DENT & SONS LTD
LONDON

DEDICATION

For Dr Joan Christison and Dr L. G.
Harper, Sisters J. Chisholm and J.
Gorman, Staff Nurse M. MacDonald,
Nurses J. Lewis, J. MacGregor and A.
MacLennan. For Jim Fraser and Male
Nurses Denis Fraser, Louis Gunn, Sandy
MacCurragh, Donald MacDonald and
Jimmie Sutherland, and for all the other
staff of Dunain House, Inverness, August
1970 to February 1971, to whom I owe
more than I can ever repay.

First published 1972

Made in Great Britain
at the
Aldine Press · Letchworth · Herts
for
J. M. DENT & SONS LTD
Aldine House · Bedford Street · London

ISBN 0 460 07866 6

Contents

Illustrations

Acknowledgments

I would like to thank all the many friends who have helped me over my two 'difficult' years (1970 and 1971). They are too numerous to list, but include Barry and Rosemary Auld, Ken and Sallie MacArthur, Miss Alice Maconochie of Inverewe, Bob and Jean Robertson, Robert, Jean and John Speirs, Ann MacDonald of Uist, Tom, Mildred, Ian and Sheena Wallace, Peter and Edna MacManus, of Derby, and the many warm-hearted folk of Torridon. I would also like to thank the editors of *The Field*, *Scots Magazine* and *Shooting Times* for agreeing to the use of some material formerly used in their pages.

L. MacNALLY

THE WARNING

The dreich winter's night grew closer
And the deer on the side of the hill
Began to move down to the forest
For the easterly wind blew chill.

As they filed down the track from the mountain
And crossed the bleak windswept moor
The oldest and weakest were trailing
The strongest were well to the fore.

Along the near edge of the forest
A disused old quarry road ran
And parked out of sight in this quarry
Stood a darkened and silent van.

As the first hind stepped into the clearing
So she dropped to the crack of a gun
And the rest of the herd, close behind her,
Wheeled around and set off at a run.

As they stopped on the moor, quite bewildered,
Another was bowled over, dead
And the rest, needing no further warning,
Turned away in a body and fled.

The deer do not turn to the woods now
From the east wind that chills to the bone
But make do with the scant safer shelter
Of hummock and peat bank and stone.

MICHAEL MacNALLY

1

Highland River

A SPARKLING Highland torrent, banks green and pleasant with early summer's foliage, long stretches of jet-black pools topped and tailed by white waterfalls.

A turgid, yellow-brown spate of water, no rocks visible to stem its irresistible progress, its voice a sullen, deep-throated boom, warning one off.

Or, in even greater contrast, its water fettered and its voice muted by ice and snow, its gorges spear-tipped in gleaming icicles and corniced by overhanging snow, a hushed almost uncanny world, despite its very real beauty, without bird-song or murmur of water over stones to break the chilly stillness of the white world.

These are only some of the changing moods of the River Tarff as I knew it, a typical Highland river rising in the chaotic desolation of the Monadhliath peat-hags and ultimately, many miles later, merging its individuality, at Fort Augustus, in the anonymity of the black waters of Loch Ness.

From early boyhood the Tarff held attraction for me. One of my earliest memories of it is of being taken to task by an elderly farmer for presuming to play with a home-made boat in the waters of its lower reaches *on a Sunday*.

Later in life I was initiated by an uncle into the art of fishing its deep pools and warned of its dangerous gorges and of its swift changes of mood. Despite this warning, oft-repeated though it was, the Tarff almost claimed me while on a fishing trip with my brother

Hugh, when we were both in our teens. We had crossed to the opposite bank to fish a difficult pool and while we were over the river suddenly began to rise. Our necessary return across it now demanded a risky jump from a steeply angled slab, already awash and treacherous, over a channel through which the rising torrent rushed to a large boulder, beyond which enough huge boulders were still exposed to form practicable stepping-stones. Hugh jumped safely, sure-footed as any mountain goat, but as I plucked up courage to follow my foot slipped from under, on the wet and slippery incline, and I was in the water from which I had so recently been plucking trout. Poetic justice, one might think, but I had no time to think. So devastatingly swift was the rushing of the rain-swollen water that my feet, as I shall always remember, did not even touch bottom. I was swept out straight as a board (or perhaps I should say 'matchstick') on the white-marbled surface of the river while with life-saving speed and presence of mind Hugh thrust out the walking stick he carried and I just managed to grab it. I was hauled out, dripping and half stunned with the suddenness of it all, while, from fifty yards or so downstream, the hollow 'boom' of a waterfall in its passage over and between fangs of rock drove home the narrowness of my escape. Had I been alone that day these words would never have seen print nor would I have experienced the coincidence of rescuing my own son, also Lea, in *his* teens, from the melting snow and rain-swollen waters of a tributary burn of the Tarff (as described in *Highland Deer Forest*) in circumstances very alike, except that then we were after deer and not trout. As it was, thanks to Hugh, I went home dripping wet but alive and, I remember, even congratulating myself that I had tied my fishing rod to my bag before I essayed the crossing and so had not lost that, as I most certainly would have done had I had it in one hand.

Flowing, as it does, from apparently sterile high-ground peat bog to cultivated low ground, the Tarff has on each side of its course a wide cross section of Highland wildlife. It begins tamely enough, the young Tarff, meandering rather sluggishly through glistening-black haggy banks for about two miles or so in surroundings of heathery hillocks and peat-black flats so austere as to seem almost forbidding. Unlikely though it may seem to the casual onlooker yet there *is* life in this monotone of heather and exposed peat. Grouse exist on the heathery islets among the peat-runners of this high-ground plateau, while teal and tufted duck appear in late spring on its infinitude of tiny black lochans. The most obvious life, of course, is in the presence of that most splendid of our Highland wildlife, the red deer, bringing animation, more particularly in summer and early autumn, to a landscape which to the superficial eye would otherwise be almost devoid of life. I have seen summering herds of stags out there, new antlers still thick in velvet, seeking peace alike from the torment of flies and humans. It was here also that I watched a 'knobber', a young staggie with still only the 'knobs' of youth on his head, almost step on a grouse which 'exploded' from below his forelegs. He made a convulsive plunge to one side and then, apparently quickly realizing that it was 'only grouse', he stood still and watched while they skimmed over the low, heathery skyline which bordered his vision. Here, too, on a day of humid summer heat when the hinds I was watching were all too obviously tormented by flies, high as they were, I saw what I thought, momentarily, were the antlers of a stag appear against the peat-black heather-topped bank some sixty yards ahead of me. And then I realized, belatedly, as a young hind rose to her feet and shook black, clinging peat droplets from her darkened hide, that it had not been antlers but the legs of the young hind, as she had rolled completely over, enjoying her beauty bath (or mud-pack, if you like) as much as any society beauty, and with more definite purpose in that her 'coat' of wet peat served, temporarily at least, in cooling her down and in rendering her immune to the stampede-inducing attentions of the flies.

The other more permanent though much less apparent inhabitant of this peaty world is the water vole, black of coat in the north, the only indication of whose presence may be the sudden, startlingly loud 'plop' as one dives into the black waters of a peat drain, in which it is immediately hidden. These voles (not to be confused with water rats) are not easily seen, seldom being far from their tunnels in the peat 'runners'. Blunt-headed, jet-black and sleek of fur and with bright orange-coloured teeth, they are vegetarians and, strange as it may seem for such a small and apparently ever-alert animal, so quick to reach concealment in either water or in the sanctuary of a peat-tunnel, they feature regularly as prey at eyries of the golden eagle in this locality.

After this relatively quiet start the juvenile Tarff, in a fit of seeming rashness prophetic of its future course, slips down a short series of rocky cascades before suddenly leaping into space in the Falls of Tarff, descending in one dizzy swoop about a hundred sheer feet.

5

As if regretting its initial rashness, however, this it does in the relative secrecy of a steep-sided rocky bowl, so that only from a certain angle, and that far away, on an opposite hill face, can this awe-inspiring swoop be admired in full.

Below this, the character of the Tarff alters completely to a boulder-strewn, relatively shallow, Highland river, while a few sparse and stunted birches begin to clothe its greener banks. A steep-sided high and narrow glen, with numerous grey rock screes striping its predominantly green slopes, Glen Tarff now confines the river at the bottom of its 'V'. In the kinder climate of the steep-sided glen we have a much more varied population of birds and animals. Strangely enough, ptarmigan seem to favour the high ground of its west side, to nest and live on, and this that most lovely and hardy of our game birds does all the year round. In contrast, another lover of the high ground of the Highlands, the greenshank, prefers the east side of the high ground above the river, and comes there only to nest and rear its young, leaving the inhospitable winter conditions of the 'tops' for the more clement conditions of the sea-coasts. Like the ptarmigan a superlatively camouflaged bird, which will sit tight and immobile while with clumsy feet the unseeing human tramples by, her nest is extremely hard to locate. Once found, however, one may well find her nest much more easy to locate in future years, for like most of our birds she uses a certain 'territory' and I have found her nesting within eight measured feet of a previous year's site.

High above the course of the river also, approximately at the 1,500-ft level, spaced out for some two miles of Glen Tarff, are no less than seven eyrie sites, all belonging to the pair of golden eagles whose territory it is. It took me years to find all of these eyries from the time my imagination was first kindled by the shepherd who assured me, without blinking an eye, 'There must be at least a cart-load of sticks in the biggest of the nests in that Glen'. Artistic licence as this undoubtedly was, the largest of the seven eyries known to me *was* huge, with a structure of heather, stalks, and dead branches six feet in height. This eyrie site was one of some antiquity, for its lower structure was compacted into a solid mass with no individual branches discernible. I last saw it in use in 1962, when it was still at its maximum height. I wrote, in my eagle notes for 1962: 'Out to look at eyries, on April 6th. After an overnight fall of snow the ground around my house was white, and the hills were covered. As I approached the first eyrie after a walk of some eight miles the

6

sun came out and in a moment the glen's garment of dull white became one of sparkling snow so bright as to hurt the eyes. So clear was the snow-reflected sunlight that I was able to pick out, from about a mile distant with my stalking "glass", that fresh structure had been added to the eyrie. My assumption that it was in use was confirmed when an eagle flew from the hill face when I was within 400 yards of the nest. A moment or so later and I saw both eagles, now high over the opposite face of the glen. As I neared the eyrie, one of the pair, the female probably, came across the glen in a fast, steep glide to pass fairly low above my head, her own head bent down in inspection of me as she flew above. One richly red-marked egg, smaller and more "pointed" at one end than is usual, lay in the middle of the eyrie's large platform, in the shallow cup, which was lined as usual with moss and great wood rush. About a foot of fresh structure had been added to the eyrie's height, green heather stalks mainly, and the egg must have only recently been laid, so "clean" did the nest cup look, with the single egg immaculate, red-brown against the green.'

This eyrie I paid periodic visits to, with more and more fore-boding, until 15th May when I wrote, 'Forebodings realized; egg cold and female had obviously given up trying to hatch it.' This egg, which proved to be only the size of a common buzzard's rather than that of the eagle, was addled and was the first sign of things going wrong with the breeding success of this pair of eagles.

Year after year I visited these eyries, but it was not until 1968 that another egg was laid by the female of this pair, and again it was not hatched. The following year, 1969, a single egg was laid on one of the other sites and this time it was hatched and the single eaglet reared successfully. This appeared to me to be the turning point for this pair and I hoped, indeed expected, to see successful breeding again annually in this glen. Vain hope it has so far turned out to be, for in 1970 and 1971 no eggs were laid in the glen, and that is the situation as I write these words, in 1971.

It was at the nest six feet high (part of which had collapsed on my 1970 visit) that I first had the almost indescribable thrill of knowing that I was only a matter of feet from a golden eagle while I heard the crunch of bones, as a grouse was rent into shreds by the female to feed her single young one. Craning out ever so slowly and cautiously to peer over the rock overhang which hid nest and occupants from me, I was immediately petrified by the outraged glare of piercing aquiline eyes as the female looked up from the grouse, firmly held down by two immense taloned feet, which she was dissecting for the eaglet, now 'cheeping' shrilly, as if in indignation, at this inter-ruption to its meal.

On an occupied eyrie of this pair wildcat kittens had once been found and I personally saw fox on more than one occasion in this same glen, as prey at the eyries. Here, too, an eagle, startled on seeing me into almost stalling in mid-air, dropped its prey in conse-quence. This proved to be a black water vole with orange chisel teeth still clamped, in a last convulsive grip, on a tuft of grass, as they had been, obviously, when death struck suddenly from the sky. Despite its small size it was not difficult to find, for the eagle had, conveniently, dropped it to land at my feet.

The scattered screes which stripe the glen here afford ideal nesting-sites for the ring-ousel, the handsome 'mountain black-bird' with its distinctive gorget of white around neck and upper breast while, lower on these same slopes, wheatears and meadow pipits nest.

Sandpipers have their own stretches of the river's edge here, all too obvious in their agitation if one is near a nest, bobbing pale breasts with a flirting of short tail, from the standpoint of a riverside rock. Grey wagtails, those most elegant and streamlined of the wag-tail family, fly in undulating wagtail flight from a nest on a ledge of riverside rock, while dumpy and maternal looking, in contrast to the wagtails' elegance, a dipper may fly, low and direct, over the river, so occupied with maternal cares that it scarcely deigns to notice one. Here, too, and indeed downward along its entire course to its end in Loch Ness, goosanders, those feathered anglers with the saw-toothed beaks, may demonstrate the ultimate in water-skiing expertise, riding the waters of the most frightful spate with consum-mate ease and obvious lack of concern.

Red deer cross from bank to bank on this upper stretch of the river almost daily, and in the high coires on each side of the Tarff many deer calves are born each June. It was on this bit that I found a deer calf recently dead, with the hind bellowing her distress in what one could imagine to be an ineffectual attempt to recall it to life. It had only been a day or so old, a tragically short spell of life for it, and it was not until I skinned it in an effort to find out how it had died that I found it had been killed by an eagle, puncture marks of talons piercing the spinal vertebrae at the middle of the back and at the base of the neck. This could only have happened in the hind's absence (probably away feeding) leaving the recently born calf lying where it was born, trusting to its instinct to remain absolutely still until the mother returned, to keep it in safety. Even this instinctive immobility, however, had not prevented its detection by the keen eyes of the eagle. Had the hind been with the calf she would have defended it from the eagle's attack; as it was she had only arrived back in time to drive the eagle from the body of her dead calf.

On the high greens bordering the river here one may see mountain hares, at one time so plentiful that in the words of a stalker of that past era 'one could be seen beside every stone'. Again a highly coloured description, but one which can give a graphic picture of how numerous the mountain hares were in those pre-1914–18 Great War days. About the mid 1920s these hares, for no apparent reason, suddenly dwindled in the north-west Highlands and they have not re-established themselves since. Yet in the north-east Highlands they are still very numerous, so much so that annual hare drives are needed to keep their numbers in check, and 'bags' of a thousand may yet be made.

The cairns of larger rock which occur among the grey screes here give sanctuary and den sites to fox, badger and, occasionally, an otter, embarking on an overland journey from one river system to another and perhaps 'lying up' en route, in a hill-side cairn.

Towards the end of what is still a relatively high ground stretch the sparse edging of birch trees and rowans changes to a bordering more thickly wooded though still mainly of birch with, occasionally, rowans and alder trees interspersed with grey willows. Entering this wooded stretch the Tarff changes in gradual transition to a narrower, rock-girt channel with, it seems, ever-deepening gorges. Here I have seen the kestrel nest and also, occasionally, the tawny owl. Not always in amity either, for I once found a scattering of plucked-out kestrel feathers on a ledge which, in that instance, was most likely to have been the work of a tawny owl.

This gorge-like aspect of the Tarff is sharply accentuated towards the end of the wooded stretch, steep, black, moisture-dripping, essentially gloomy cliff walls, enclosing deep black pools. So essentially gloomy is this stretch that I was once inspired to remark to a rather talkative 'rifle' I had out stalking that it was a perfect place for a murder. Glancing up from where he was rather apprehensively skirting the edge of the Stygian gorge to where I was looming above

9

him, his chatter suddenly dried up and I fancy he regarded me with some doubt for the rest of that day.

A brief but very welcome respite comes as the gloomy gorge of the Black Wood (as the wood here is called from the descriptive Gaelic) opens out to the kindlier greens at the confluence of a big tributary burn (the Allt Lagain a'bhainne) with the main river. A green, meadow-like flat, much of it now overgrown by rushes, marks the spot where, in the old pastoral days, the people had their summer shielings. Roughly translated *Lagain a'bhainne* means 'the hollow, or flat, of the milk', while its alternative title, to the old folk, is still 'the dairy glen'.

The welcome green and pleasant aspect of the Tarff is of brief duration, however, for very shortly after it the gorge-like aspect of its former course is again renewed in a succession of steep-sided cliffs with white water at head and tail of long, black pools, interspersed very briefly by shallower stretches of rock-strewn waters. The river continues thus for some four miles, much of its course quite inaccessible, overhung by wet, weeping walls, rankly 'scented' in summer by the 'wild garlic' which grows wherever there is sufficient soaking soil to hold it. Ironically enough it is at the bottom of one of the inaccessible gorges, with rock so overhanging that it is difficult even to *see* it, that a 'natural' bridge exists, rock joining rock right across the narrow bottom of a chasm. Below this 'saddle' of rock the black waters vanish, in normal water, into the circular void of a hole in the rock. 'Bridge' and hole alike vanish when the river is in spate, lost under the depth of pent-up foaming water confined by the narrow walls of rock.

Above these depressing black cliffs, which so often hide the river here from the path which runs above it, are, however, very pleasant green banks, well clad in birch, rowan, hazel, birdcherry and alder, with an occasional ash, elm, or grey willow to add more variety. In spring the freshness of the new greens provides an ever-reviving boost to a spirit dulled by a long leafless winter, especially so after heavy overnight rain has cleared to a dewy morning, leaving the banks redolent with the heady incense of fresh-bruised young birch leaves. In summer the green foliage becomes over-heavy, its freshness lost to an eye satiated with green so that its replacement by the vivid tints of autumn is welcomed anew, even though it is prophetic of the leafless time to come so soon after.

In late spring and throughout early summer these banks are

10

athrong with a still richer variety of bird life than in the river's higher reaches. Willow warblers with their plaintively sweet song (which typifies spring to me much more than the 'first cuckoo' so often exclaimed about) flit from branch to branch. Wood warblers, less easily seen, instantly proclaim their identity when the clear, ringing notes of their descending scale are heard. Chaffinches with their camouflaged, deep-cupped nest, an adornment to the lichen-covered trees they may nest in. Wrens with their startlingly loud, 'sudden' song coming from a bird so small. Great tits with their insistent blacksmith's anvil notes, blue tits, coal tits and long-tailed tits, all intent on securing mates or in the flurry of nest building and young-rearing which follows. Tree creepers, 'creeping' with furtive swiftness up, up, the creviced bark of a tree, now in sight, now hidden behind it. Robins, cheery as always with the warm vermilion of their breasts; missel thrushes, earliest of the thrushes to nest and almost on a par with the chaffinch as a master in the art of camouflaging its nest, with that loudly churring alarm note which typifies that dauntlessness of spirit which causes this boldly spotted thrush to pursue even a raiding sparrowhawk. Song thrushes (nicer still, the old name of 'mavis') with bright eggs laid on the smooth perfection of the nest's mud-cemented lining. Blackbirds with eggs of duller green and nest with plebeian lining of dry grass, redstarts appearing and disappearing with a flick of that chestnut red tail, all are present and all are welcome. Cuckoos flit, hawklike, in mute reflection of their parasitic nature, while, truly hawklike in dashing style and rakish appearance, the sparrowhawk dashes momentarily across the scene, singling out a victim with its cold, yellow-gold eye and carrying it away, shrieking, in its needle-sharp talons.

Birdsong, gradually diminishing as the summer moves on, becomes almost non-existent as the fading autumn foliage flares forth momentarily before dying. Families of all species of tits then unite together with a few tree creepers and gold-crest wrens, an endless 'see-see-seeing' being heard as they search the leafless trees. Flocks of field-fares and redwings arrive overnight to denude all available rowan trees of their flamboyant waxy berries and, making south, skeins of garrulous geese seem at times to use the river's course as a guide on their journey.

In these wooded banks, coming quietly up to skirt an inaccessible stretch of river, one day while fishing, I almost trod upon a sleeping fox, almost touching it before it awoke. A lightning-swift appraisal

11

coincident with an equally swift departure left me in no doubt of its views on the human race in general and on myself in particular.

Towards the end of this series of gorges one comes to Tor na Brochd which, translated from the again descriptive Gaelic, means the 'ridge of the badger'. Here, it is said, appeared the first badger sett known of in the area. The sett is still there and still used by the badgers, for it was below its many holes that, again while fishing, I saw my first badger, dead unfortunately, a drowning accident it seemed, for it was in the shallows at the river's edge that I found it.

Farther down still, the Tarff bisects a rugged, seam-marked crag known as the Raven's Rock, on which, on one side or the other, ravens have nested for generations. Usually inaccessible from above, or indeed from any angle, except by skilled and daring 'ropework', the practice in the old days was to 'blatter the young ones with a rifle' from whichever bank was opposite. Ravens are still there, however, while most of their 'blatterers' are gone, and around them, in noisy 'chack-chacking' company, nest a colony of jackdaws, arriving in February and going away again in November. The common buzzard also nests in tree or cliff site along this later stretch of the river, its bulky nest too obvious for its own good, in days gone by, when the only predator with the 'right' to kill was man himself.

That evil spirit of the hills, the grey-cloaked hooded crow, nests almost from one end of the river's course to the other, the only criterion being that it must have a tree to nest in, though even this, it appears, is not invariable, for an acquaintance from Central Perthshire once found a nest of hoodies in the heather, after he had searched every tree in the vicinity and roundly damned his neighbour for giving sanctuary to the pair of hoodies he knew was in the area. Among the many fine bird photographs which the late Ian M. Thompson took in his day, when bulky, heavy cameras and impedimenta added to the difficulties of this photography, are those of ground-nesting hooded crows, taken in Shetland: 'where this photograph was taken there are no trees and the hooded crow nests on the ground'. Of the hooded crow I can say nothing good, for it despoils nests of other species, from golden eagle to yellowhammer, and victimizes any weak or sickly animal it can find, not by killing it 'cleanly' but, as a preliminary, removing its eye (or eyes if it can get at both) before pecking and pulling at any bit of exposed flesh, through wool or hair, until its victim is beyond all aid. Perhaps its only redeeming feature is that it has clung to existence in the face of the most rigorous persecution man could devise over the past century. Strangely for a bird which has done this, its bulky nest, usually built before the trees are in leaf, is easily detected, needing only the time, energy and will to search for it, and even more oddly, the species seems to have a liking for a particular area of trees, which means that with knowledge of this trait one can concentrate the search in that area.

The Tarff is now rapidly approaching the lower arable ground through, in one particular stretch, a concentration of hazel trees on each side, in which roe deer, Japanese sika deer and, occasionally, a red squirrel can be seen. After passing through this last stretch the river widens into a relatively shallow, boulder-strewn course and retains this character until it merges with Loch Ness. Rabbits were at one time numerous about this last stretch but are now, since the vile, man-induced scourge of myxomatosis, almost non-existent. Where the river passed through the marginal land, on the borders of the 'hill' and arable ground, a professional rabbit-trapper used to be employed in autumn and winter. Among the hundreds of rabbits which this trapper would catch in trap or snare there were, annually, a catch of a dozen to fourteen or so wildcats, 'accidentally' caught while after rabbits along runs or at burrows. Now, since the rabbit has gone, the wildcat has also dwindled there and one is lucky to get an occasional sighting of one in a year. Deserved as is the reputation for 'wildness', or should we say 'independence', of spirit of the wildcat, that for aggressiveness and ferocity for ferocity's sake alone is, in my experience, equally undeserved. The wildcat will defend itself or its kittens, using both teeth and the sharp claws of all four legs, but attack without reason, no.

Badgers, to my mind, are increasing and spreading in many parts of the Highlands and, on a bank near the Tarff's last 'tame' stretch, there is now a badger sett in enlarged holes which were sure to have held rabbits in my youth at Fort Augustus. This sett is only about 800 yards from the nearest house and yet, nocturnal as the badger is, few people have seen one in the flesh.

Near its journey's end at Loch Ness the Tarff is even wider and now placid, a Highland river 'tamed', but for those *not* 'tamed' in spirit the wildness of its upper stretches remains alluring and, I trust, will always do so.

2

The Hummel's Last Rut

HUMMEL stags are usually permanently antlerless. By reason of some defect in the pedicles (the 'roots' on the red deer skull from which the antlers grow annually) the hummel is denied the branching adornment which lends attraction and dignity to the typical red deer stag. They have long aroused interest and speculation because of this. Here is a stag with the apparent handicap of no antlers, in an antlered race, which can nevertheless achieve sufficient success in besting antlered rivals at the red deer rut, and thus acquiring hinds.

Indeed, due to the fact that hummels *can* be successful in this, a legend has grown up of their invincibility. They have been credited with invariably growing to gigantic size and with, just as invariably, soundly defeating all their antlered rivals.

The truth is rather less romantic for, while it is logical to suppose that if hummels manage to avoid being shot as 'undesirables' until they reach full maturity, they *should* weigh heavier than their contemporaries who have an annual drain in regrowing antlers, I have never seen a hummel of gigantic or even exceptional size. Probably relatively few hummels do attain full maturity in body weight; most of the dozen or so I have stalked were below eight years of age and the oldest and heaviest weighed only a trifle over sixteen stone, a good weight but not exceptional in Highland stags, nor one likely to confer invincibility. I have watched hummels 'challenging' and 'defending', and emerging as victor or vanquished

14

in pretty well equal proportions. I would say, in fact, that they have an even chance in rutting contests with antlered stags, the crux of the matter being the weight of the combatants, and, this being equal, (as happens rarely) the 'heart' and agility of the contenders for marital status.

One could admire the courage of the hummel in taking on adversaries having the weapons of antlers which he lacks if one did not suspect, unromantic as it may be, that this courage is rather the unreasoning compulsion of the red deer rut, which is such an apparent feature in all red deer stags at that time. Courage or un-reasoning compulsion, there is no doubt he suffers some heavy drubbings in his fighting, for almost every hummel I have skinned has borne evidence of this in bruises and gashes over his body. A feature peculiar to rutting stags as the mating season gets into full swing is the physical evidence of their 'serving' of hinds in that the inside of their haunches becomes progressively bruised in the actual 'impact' of their rough mating. This the hummel stag exhibits also, so that he most definitely serves hinds, though one of the theories at times aired to account for his antlerless state is 'damage to, or lack of, testes'. I have always made a point of checking this in all hummels shot and there was never any evidence of it. They were 'normal' in every way except that the bony excrescences, known as pedicles, present on the skulls of the typical red deer stags, from which the antlers grow, were only mere rudimentary 'bumps' of bone, in some cases almost non-existent.

One-antlered stags are, in effect, 'half-hummels' in that the pedicle on their antlerless side is also rudimentary. An intriguing cause for surmise arises in a one-antlered stag with six good points on his only antler (we had two at Culachy while I was there). Was the sire a hummel, or a royal? Had his dam hummel or royal blood? And how fascinating to see that the 'struggle' between the un-desirable hummel type and the desirable royal strain had resulted in a 'half-hummel-royal'.

I must confess I am a firm, if unscientific, believer in transmittable tendencies in red deer antlers, having seen certain examples in my years at Culachy, but the subject is so obviously very involved and with such tremendously varied mutations under 'wild' condi-tions that it would be as unwise to dogmatize about it as indeed about most matters of wildlife. This much I have read, as a record of the probable undesirability of hummels as 'bad breeders', in *Hunting and Stalking the Deer* by Lionel Edwards and H. F. Wallace:

'Captain Donne, author of *Game Animals of New Zealand*, writes: "I have definite information of a hummel stag, in Scotland, being enclosed with hinds one rut. Three male calves were eventually produced, one was a hummel, one was a one-antlered stag, the third a stag with malformed antlers."'

I had opportunity here one season to watch a hummel's progress at the rut and from this direct observation and partly from surmise built up on circumstantial evidence I wrote the following.

Dusk was beginning to mask the October hills, hills now noisy with the roaring of the rutting, rampaging stags, as the hummel stag crossed into what was, to him, unknown territory. Though still big-framed he was past his prime and he was very tired. For a fortnight now he had roared and raged on what had been his 'home' territory, until the bitter, inevitable lesson had been learned, that he was no longer capable of holding hinds against younger, more vigorous, antlered stags. Again and again he had got together hinds, holding them at times for days, at others for hours only, but always a stag still in full prime of weight and strength had usurped his 'ownership', though never without a struggle. And so he was now wandering, seeking his fortune elsewhere, urged on by that demoniac unrest which possesses red stags at the rut. Lacking the antlers which lend distinction to the appearance of most stags he had nevertheless a leonine mane as thick and shaggy as any antlered beast. His head, with only its two dark, curly-hair-covered knobs, was strikingly grey and he was distinctly 'Roman-nosed'. Altogether, he lacked attraction to the eye used to antlered stags; there was something repulsive and bestial about his uncrowned head as he raised it to roar his unrest in the gathering darkness.

For an hour yet he journeyed on, pausing only to roar at intervals, until he was deep into strange ground. Hinds there were in plenty and often he lingered near the fringe of a herd, only to travel on again as a stag which his new-found discretion warned him carried 'too much metal' for him, came from his harem to 'see him off'.

At last, above a scattered birch wood, he found a small herd of hinds and with them, by good fortune, only a three-year-old staggie. This over-ambitious stripling he forthwith summarily dethroned, and rounding up his new-won herd he drove them, a huge, chest-

16

heavy 'sheep dog', farther down towards the birches. Higher in the gloom of the hill a resounding roar spoke of the presence of a big stag, holding hinds also, and the hummel desired no such dangerous proximity in the hours of darkness.

Tired as he was, and still sore from a recently acquired antler-stab in one flank, which he had been too slow to avoid when he had had to flee after one of his fruitless contests, he gave himself little rest that night, the ferment of having hinds keeping him ceaselessly rounding them, roaring almost without pause. Once the deposed staggie tried to sneak in and 'cut out' some hinds, only to be discovered as the hinds scattered before him, and chased savagely out over the dark hill. Returning after his grunting wrath had expended itself, the hummel found that a 'knobber', a yearling male, had seized the opportunity to rejoin his mother with whom he had still been until the jealousy of the rut had evicted him. He, too, was unceremoniously thrown out, to linger about disconsolately, but at a discreet distance from the herd of which he had been a member.

At daybreak the hummel 'refreshed' himself by wallowing in a black and odorous peat hole, much frequented of late as its hoof-scarred edges bore witness. This he first stirred to a porridge-like consistency with a flailing forefoot before subsiding into it, first on one side, then on the other, luxuriating in it, rubbing head and neck blissfully along its drier edge. When he eventually emerged he too was peat-black and odorous, an intimidating sight in his dripping blackness, only his grey head and mane free of the clinging garment of wet peat. An erratic, weaving circuit, around and amid his hinds, who scattered warily at his approach, assured him that all was secure. He lay down to doze fitfully, jerking to wakefulness at every faintly heard roar, only to drowse again as he realized that the roarer was far away. The hinds, too, lay down, one by one, and began placidly to chew their cuds; they, too, had had a restless night, with the constant chivvying of the hummel, but for all that they had managed to fill their bellies, which was more than could be said for their lord and master.

Some two hours later, now wakeful, he was alerted by the sudden fixed stare, rigid in wide-eared attention, of a nearby hind. A moment she lay thus and then rose to her feet for one more long, intent look down among the birches before her muffled bark stilled the cud-chewing of her sisters and brought them to their feet, to follow her gaze. Another gruff bark, more definite this time, and away they all trotted while the hummel, after an abortive attempt to stop their retreat, lumbered in their rear.

They had gone some way before he succeeded in heading them off, and, working round them, brought them to an uneasy halt. Most of the herd had no inkling of what had aroused the leading hind's suspicion and so were quite ready to halt, until her suspicions were confirmed or allayed.

In the birches behind a rather rueful would-be photographer put the lens cap back on his telephoto lens. It had seemed so easy, an approach masked by the trees and a chance of some photographs, but one slightly incautious move and the keen-eyed hind had got him. He sat back and viewed the stationary herd through his tele-scope, working out a new line of approach if they settled, as now seemed probable. Farther out another herd was visible on a skyline, a big, antlered stag roaring his 'ownership'. The hummel was anxious to prevent his hinds from working out any farther in that direction, for any intermingling of the two herds must immediately lead to a trial by force, and that he could not afford.

As the interested onlooker continued to watch, first one hind, then another began to lie down, with the hummel standing, watchful, on their upper edge. All seemed well. Then from out of a hollow on the flanking hillside, tardily alerted by a stray whiff of 'scent' from the unseen watcher, there ran in a hind and calf, pursued by an antlered stag of about the hummel's size, but redder of coat and 'fresher' looking. The hind and calf ran into the herd of the hummel, *their* stag too far behind to stop this, and the hummel at once left his herd and advanced to meet the newcomer. Fully 200 yards he paced and as he neared it so did the antlered stag turn away slightly and begin to pace, in a wide arcing circuit, around the again uneasy hinds. The hummel likewise turned and, all the time keeping between the inter-loper and his hinds, paced stiff-legged stride for stride with him, keeping very slightly ahead and parallel to the stranger's circuit. Their silent, ritualistic 'two step', fraught with unvoiced menace, carried on for about one hundred and fifty yards, drains being jumped in circus-horse unison as they came to them; all the time the hummel maintained his distance from the focal point of his hinds and thereby kept the incomer, on the outer circuit, well away from them. Suddenly, as if an invisible barrier had snapped, they were at each other with panther-like agility, the hummel wheeling like lightning to engage the incomer while he was equally quick in lowering his antlered head to receive him. Head to head they met, antlered and antlerless, and then began the usual plunging, heaving, pushing match, with quick wheels and short, plunging rushes as each strove to push the other back. The photographer watched enthralled as the struggle raged up and down the hillside, then, recollecting his wits, realized he might get up to them and get a photo, they seemed so evenly matched. Rising to his feet, the need now for haste, not concealment, he began to run across, the hinds vanishing at his appearance, the combatants engrossed in their own struggle paying no heed, as indeed he had banked on. Run as hard as he could, he was yet only half-way when the issue was settled; the hummel, vanquished again by a younger opponent, disengaged and ran precipitately while the victor pursued him a few yards thrusting and hooking viciously at the retreating haunches. Downhill the hummel came, towards the birches once more while his conqueror turned to reap the fruits of his victory only to find that he, too, was bereft, for by now the disturbed hinds had 'run into' the herd held by the big stag higher up, and with him there was no disputing ownership.

The disappointed photographer, now crouched behind a low knoll, watched the hummel approach and saw him sniff longingly at the 'beds' where his hinds had lain, lifting Roman-nosed head in the air and wrinkling nose and lips in a grotesque, lewd-seeming grimace as if in reminiscence as a particularly 'attractive' scent regaled him.

For a few moments he sniffed around thus and then began to walk in the direction of the photographer, stopping to roar half-heartedly at intervals. A bogus 'roar' from the watcher halted him and then brought him to a cautious advance on the unseen roarer. And so he was photographed, the 'click' of the camera alerting him, puzzling in its alien metallic sharpness, and sending him away again, but only slowly, his habitual keenness of senses numbed by his rutting fever.

For most of the remainder of the day the bereft hummel wandered around, now into the lower ground where there were few deer. In mid-afternoon he 'lay-up' for a couple of hours of uneasy rest and as evening approached rose stiffly and resumed his ceaseless quest. In this he was at last rewarded in finding a small family party of three, an old hind, her calf and her yearling hind grazing together in bracken and birches very near to the arable ground. With them he settled for the night, his roaring heard by the estate stalker as he went to bed that night, and again as he rose in the morning.

Still early, on that morning, as the old hind grazed amid the withering brown of the brackens, screened from view by the autumn gold of the birches, a crackle of trodden-upon bracken sent her head up in swift inquiry. One look was sufficient and off she led, her family's departure revealed by their movement now to the stalker approaching from below. He watched them go, enjoying the swinging ease of gait with which they took the hill. The old hind had been about there with her family for some time now and he had half-expected to see them. What he had *not* expected was the sight of the big hummel lumbering at the rear of the party and it was with a half-stifled imprecation that he reached, too late, for the rifle slung on his back. Hummels were undesirables to him, for he believed that they were bad breeding stock, and in any case they lacked the attraction of the antlered stags. Making up his mind, he began to follow them up as they went, the hummel all unconscious that he was now the object of a pursuit more deadly than that of photography.

Reaching the ridge top above the bracken and birches the stalker sat down to spy ahead. There they were, now about a mile distant, the hummel stopped, broadside, conspicuous in his 'blackness', the light-coloured hind family blending in with the hill's autumn tint, and still walking out, though slower now, picking a bite here and there. Up towards the skyline of a higher distant ridge ahead they were making, and the hummel, after his momentary pause to survey the ground they had left, carried on behind them. Near to the skyline there lay a small herd of 'knobbers', cast out from the herds to which their various mothers belonged by the stags 'in charge' who tolerated no males above the age of calfhood in their harems. They lay together still slightly bewildered by the enforced separation which the rut had brought and yet with a slow stirring yeast of male instincts awakening as the fever of the rut began to infect them. Close by grazed a lone hind, a straggler, overlooked from a herd the previous night, and the hummel added her to his small party, glad of any 'crumb' as he went by. The biggest 'knobber', more forward in his awakening instincts than the others, took umbrage at this, no doubt deeming in his youthful inexperience that the hummel was just another of his kind. In this he was speedily disabused, for having trotted over belligerently, one contemptuous hard dunt from the hummel's grey poll shattered conclusively his ambitions and aspirations; far behind, the stalker grinned appreciatively at the small by-play.

One by one the hummel's small party topped the skyline, his black form being last to vanish. Far in the rear came the stalker, secure in the knowledge that from the ridge he could command enough ground to pick them up again.

Once over the top, the strong breeze blowing full in their noses, the hummel's party quickened pace. A further mile away over the burn at the foot of the long slope and midway up the opposite one was a widely scattered herd of hinds. To this herd the old hind belonged and to it she was now returning. Reigning over most of this herd there was a strong eight-pointer, confident in his vigorous prime, and as he saw the oncoming party he roared a warning and, as they drew near, raced out and quickly drove the hinds to among his own herd. The hummel did not stop to argue, but astutely weighing up the possibilities of the wide-scattered hinds, he ran on westwards and adroitly 'cut out' a dozen or so, driving them, without a halt, on before him. Again the watcher behind had reason to grin appreciatively, though without altering his designs on the big hummel.

The hummel drove them a respectable distance from the main herd before he stopped, then, a herd-owner again by a further twist of the wheel of fortune, he showed his authority by chivvying his hinds about as they tried to graze. His vigour restored, he roared incessantly and at intervals made grunting sorties at some neighbouring staggies, hopeful hangers-on in the proximity of the large herd of hinds.

Watching patiently until it became obvious that the hummel had really 'settled down', the stalker then began to make an approach which took him the best part of an hour, the last bit being a cautious wriggle up the burn and a belly-flat slither to a hummock some one hundred and sixty yards from the herd of the hummel. Most of the hinds were lying now, cudding, much of their bodies concealed in the tussocky 'white-grass', but their gaze commanding a wide vista below them.

The hummel (maliciously, the stalker thought) chose to lie down just as the possible firing point was reached, completely masked by a low swell in the ground. The prone watcher resigned himself to a long wait, assured by his 'command' of most of the hinds that he must sooner or later get his chance at their overlord. It was, in fact, over an hour later before renewed roaring from the eight-pointer awoke the dozing hummel. Another stag, far to the west, joined in the roaring and the hummel, unable to rest any longer, rose to his feet. The top of his back and his grey head appeared above the concealing 'swell' as he chivvied the only hind still on her feet forward a little. Then characteristically averse to seeing his hinds at peace he advanced to stand among them, in full view now. Neck outstretched to roar, all his weight carried forward in shaggy neck and deep chest, falling away to tucked-up looking loins, he did not hear the shot that closed his years on the hill, or see the departure of his hinds to whom it meant yet another change of ownership in the kaleidoscope of their life at the rut.

For the old hummel the unrest and frustration of his last rut were over while yet the bitterness of waning powers, to one who had known 'better days', had barely been fully realized.

3

Beauty, a Red Deer Calf

'BEAUTY' came to us, literally, on 7th June 1959, and it happened thus. On the day in question I was walking quietly through the hill when I suddenly became aware of a red deer hind, some distance away. She was quite alone apparently, and very obviously a thin, ageing hind, her poor condition evident in her tufty, harsh-looking coat and in her sharp-looking hip-bones and spinal ridge. Seeing her alone like that I at once suspected that she was an old hind, worn out by age and at the end of her tether. The other possible solution, that she had a recently born calf lying nearby, I discounted at once; so poor a hind could not possibly rear and give suck to a calf, greedy in its demands for milk. A moment or two later, however, as a tiny 'black-looking' red deer in miniature struggled to its feet and stood swaying weakly beside the old hind, I had to accept the solution I had rejected. She had indeed a calf, poor and weak-looking as she was. I was a scant four hundred yards away when she at last noticed me. Momentarily she stood her ground, then she moved hesitantly away a few steps, stopped, retraced them, nuzzled at the calf, then threw her head up, regarded my advancing figure fixedly with ears cocked and sensitive nostrils aflare before turning to run, this time in real earnest, vanishing in the labyrinth of peat hags which the coire held.

Watching her departure I had taken my eyes off the calf (as I was in all probability meant to do) and when I looked again it too had vanished. Although I had its locality pretty well pinpointed it nevertheless took me some time to relocate the tiny calf, in the long heather where it had dropped and in which it now lay, not really a 'beauty' at that very early stage in its life, with damp and matted hair dark with moisture, on which the dapples, which so enhance the irresistible appeal of the young red deer calf, or roe deer fawn, were as yet barely visible. Her (for it was a female calf) little hooves, so definitely black and sharp-edged in later life, were yellow-white and 'plastic' to the touch, the edges of their cleats ragged in appearance, not at all 'clean-cut' as they so shortly would be when the calf, as it rapidly grew stronger, had spent some hours on its legs.

As I sat there pondering, wondering whether so poor a hind could rear such a weak-looking calf or whether it would shortly become one of the very few, relatively speaking, red deer calves which die 'naturally', my mind was made up for me as the calf again rose on unsteady legs and swayed across the few yards which separated us, to prod weakly at my seated figure as if in mute appeal. Though I knew perfectly well that her damp nose was merely investigating my jacket pocket for an illusory milk-teat, I was lost then. Guilty as I felt over depriving even such a travesty of a hind of her calf I knew that her sense of loss would not last long and I tried to absolve myself with the fact that the odds were against the calf's survival if I left it. I knew that I could supply it with plenty of milk anyway, whereas it was uncertain that the mother could.

I carried 'Beauty', a title she most definitely deserved when a few more hours of life had dried out her charmingly dappled red-brown coat, most of the way home. At intervals, over the apparently lengthening miles, I put her down and let her slowly follow me, already accepted as her 'mother', while my aching arms got a rest. Light as she was I was very thankful when I could at last put her down and listen to the delighted exclamation of Margaret, my wife, when she saw my foundling.

At her first feed Beauty proved to be more hungry than competent in sucking milk from a rubber teat, contriving somehow to squirt more milk over me than went down her throat. As her periodic feeds grew in number, however, so did she rapidly gain in competence and she was soon sucking lustily four times daily, so lustily in fact that once or twice she pulled the teat right off the makeshift bottle, which again resulted in my getting more than my fair share of the milk.

I 'lodged' Beauty in a conveniently empty kennel within sight and

A hen sparrowhawk at her nest in the wooded banks of the River Tarff.

Red deer stags in summer velvet on the high ground where the Tarff begins its course to Loch Ness.

Red deer cross the upper reaches of the Tarff almost daily.

Golden eagle on eyrie, high above the River Tarff.

Foxes' den up in cairns of rock on the high ground in the Highlands.

The wildcat will defend itself by using tooth and claw.

A hummel stag, repulsive in aspect to those of us who prefer red deer stags to be antlered.

A young Japanese Sika stag in the 'black' coat of winter.

Blue hares are scarce in the north-west Highlands nowadays.

VI

Hummel stags are usually permanently antlerless and thus lack attraction for most of us.

Grouse inhabit the heathery high ground.

A pair of badgers about to commence their night's foraging.

VIII

scent of my terriers. This may seem strange to my readers, but having dogs about the house and out with me so often I *had* to get both Beauty and the dogs well accustomed to each other, though I little dreamt in those early days that Beauty would eventually win such ascendancy over the dogs as to 'flail' them away from their daily ration of biscuits with one shrewish forefoot so that *she* could enjoy their biscuits. In any case, from the very first, when I fed Beauty, my dogs accompanied me and they rapidly learnt that she was 'mine' and was therefore 'untouchable'. At nights she went into a large kennel the entrance to which I enlarged for her. This she used during the day, too, when the sun or the midges got too much for her, so that it used to amaze visitors to see a large deer calf emerge from a 'dog's' kennel, with yapping terriers separated from her only by a thin, netting fence and indeed, latterly, when I knew she was 'safe', emerging from the same 'kennel' as herself.

In this grassed-over yard, then, she spent her first few weeks of life, supplementing her four feeds of milk daily by beginning to pluck experimentally at the grass at a fortnight old, thereafter grazing increasingly until it was more the milk supplementing her grazing than vice versa.

As she grew older I let her out to graze around my house and to accompany the dogs and myself, morning and evening, on our daily walks. She also accompanied the whole family when we 'went to the hill' on our Sunday picnics. The freedom of around the house and of the open gate to the hill she never abused, seldom going more than a few hundred yards in her grazing, coming back regularly at midday to be by the kennel gate, in nearness to her juvenile rearing-place, to chew her cud, jaws busily and rhythmically chewing, a lump vanishing down her throat and, moments later, another lump magically materializing, travelling up the length of her neck, to start her jaws' rhythmic motion once more. At night she always returned to this gate, from her afternoon's foraging, to wait until she was let in to her yard, where she had her 'last bottle' at around ten o'clock. If there was a field near to my house in which she wanted to graze, rather than go to the 'hill' behind my house, she would stand by its gate and 'bleat' until it was opened for her, similarly giving notice when she wanted to return to her midday cud-chewing area. If her milk-feed was overdue she would use the same call for it, and she would parade up and down outside the house until her needs were satisfied.

When she was little more than six weeks old, a well-grown leggy calf, still attractively dappled, she went on holiday to my brother's, who also lived in a lonely house in the hills. He came for us with a Land Rover and it was a Land Rover with a very crowded and assorted cargo in it which left Culachy. Luggage, groceries, a springer spaniel, Penny, with whom Beauty had effected an alliance, my small son Lea (eight years old) and Beauty, ensconced on my lap as there was no other place for her. The boniness of the red deer's leg became sharply obvious to me on that twelve-mile journey, as also the fact that deer refuse to be 'house-trained', a fact emphasized as I felt the first dampness leak through my kilt from where Beauty was ensconced, comfortably for her, but increasingly uncomfortably for me.

It was while on holiday at Hugh's that I nearly lost her, while still in calfhood, to a river in spate, a fatality that is always a danger to 'wild' calves when still in their early weeks of life, for if a mother hind is badly alarmed near such a river and her way of retreat is across it, cross it she will and can, but her young calf, though following without hesitation into the raging waters, at times may be carried away and drowned. I have more than once found deer calves, in those perilous first few weeks of life, drowned, in such a situation as to point to the above circumstances. In this case my eight-year-old son was becoming keen on fishing and so I took him to the nearby river, with Beauty tailing us up, grazing for minutes whenever a 'sweet bite' caught her fancy, being left behind, then running, already in 'fluid' deer motion, to catch up.

The river was high and I kept a close eye on my boy, excited as only a small boy can be, at catching his first trout. At a deep narrow pool his hook became stuck on a boulder near the edge but in some three feet of rushing water. As I tried to get it free with a long stick, Beauty, racing up from a particularly tasty bite which had beguiled her, saw me down at the river's edge, jumped from off the low bank above to join me and landed in the swiftly flowing river. She was at once swept off her feet and carried, backwards, into the deeper water beyond the boulder. Making a frantic, unthinking leap into the thigh-deep water between shore and boulder, I *just* managed to grab her as the outside of the huge boulder momentarily stayed her progress. Hauling her dripping weight over the slippery stones to the river's edge I half heaved, half pushed her up the bank, where she immediately began to graze, quite unperturbed by her, to me anyway, narrow escape. I suppose she *might* have got out herself

26

after getting out of the full force of the current but only if she'd escaped being knocked senseless by the succession of ridges of rock over which the river foamed in its rain-swollen passage. For the second time on that holiday I had a soaking kilt because of Beauty. I vowed I would wear a pair of trousers on the journey home.

Growing rapidly in independence and size Beauty began to lose her former habit of following me everywhere and, at times, especially if in a lazy, cud-chewing-induced semi-torpor, would just lie on drowsily, to catch me up at times maybe a mile from home. The one sure way still of ensuring her presence from the start was to let the dogs out. Racing out of the kennel yard, barking in delighted excitement at the prospect of a walk, they invariably aroused Beauty to a similar if less vociferous pitch and off they would all rush away ahead of me, dogs and deer calf, to come rushing back and thereafter keep more sedately with me, their initial excitement quietened down. Beauty had by this time attained complete ascendancy over the dogs. She would often now indulge in wild games of 'tig' with one unlucky terrier, singling it out unerringly for pursuit no matter how hard it tried to mix with its fellows, dabbing out with a wicked front hoof whenever she was within range, until the tormented dog eventually eluded her, or, cornered against fence or rock, sank back on its haunches, snarling and snapping impotently at its tormenter. *Her* head was always held high, ears folded back shrewishly on it, the only thing in range of the victim's snaps and lunges being the hard, polished sharp-edged hoof. It flicked out like lightning itself, demonstrating in some manner as to how a mother hind would defend her 'new' calf from any predator unlucky enough to doubt the strength of her maternal feeling.

By her first September, when about three months of age, Beauty began to assume her first winter coat, its darker thickness replacing the thin summer coat with its juvenile dapples. In early November she followed me to the hill, although on this occasion I did not take any dogs. After following well for at least three miles she began to lag behind, becoming slower and slower until she at last stopped and simply stood, looking after me. On open ground as we were then I carried on for several hundred yards before looking back at her. When I did look back it was to see that she was retracing her steps. Call and coax as I did she would not come any farther and so, anxious that she might either go astray, or was feeling sick, I in turn retraced my steps. We had returned about halfway home when the weather suddenly, and for my part completely unexpectedly, worsened. A hard-driven squally snow-shower, first of a succession of such, caught us up and made me glad I was not heading *into* it. I still wonder if a change in temperature or air pressure, imperceptible to my 'dulled' senses, had forewarned Beauty or the imminence of bad weather, or if she had merely decided, wilfully, to return home.

Beauty proved almost omnivorous in her tastes as far as vegetation went, not to mention various brands of dog-biscuits. Ivy leaves, flowers and shoots of my heretofore thriving rambler roses, various weeds such as groundsel, chickweed, dandelion and greater hawkbit, all were sampled and eaten with apparent relish. Bracken and fern tips were also sampled but eaten very sparsely. In her first autumn we had an 'acorn year' and the heavy acorn crop, littering the ground below the oaks, was discovered, tasted experimentally, and then, a new 'taste' experienced, eaten with relish. When green, growing vegetation became inevitably scarce, in her first winter, she discovered that the grey-green, hair-like lichen plentifully bedecking the older birches and oaks made a palatable substitute and with the onset of harder weather near to December's beginning, I was giving her small amounts of corn and hay, though she was not really keen on either at that early age. She was still 'on milk' but by now down to three, instead of four, bottles daily. In the first week of January she began to refuse one or other of her thrice-daily feeds of milk but still took at least two bottles, or about three pints of milk, daily.

Coinciding with a spell of hard frost, a sudden attack of 'flu put me to bed towards January's end. Whether by coincidence or not, on the very first day I was out of action, Beauty would not take *any* of her bottles. On the second day she again refused them, though (as I could hear even up in my misery in bed) she 'bleated' continually at the front of the house. My wife began to get worried and, when I was obviously feeling better on the third day of my 'flu, she told me what was happening. Beauty had, for the third successive day, refused all milk feeds and was now lying lethargically in front of the house. I muffled myself up as if planning an Arctic expedition and went out to see if *I* could persuade her to drink some milk, but again she refused. I lifted her up, no mean armful by this time, groggy as I was still feeling, and carried her into a spare stall in the stables by my house. Mixing warmed milk with that Highland standby, whisky, I took it out and with the aid of a spoon succeeded in spilling more down her throat than on my own knees. In the evening I gave her more warmed milk in this way, with some crushed aspirin in it. For five long anxious days she ate nothing, existing only on the milk I managed to force-feed her with, lying lethargically in the stall. Then, going in early on the sixth day I was surprised and delighted to see her on her legs, poking with her nose at the boards which held her in the stall. I tried her with her usual bottle and she sucked a little, not much but a tremendous advance on the force-feeding with a spoon. It was a mild day outside and as she was obviously keen to get out I eventually acceded to her unspoken request and let her out about midday. Just as soon as she got out she began to graze, picking here and there at the grass around the house. From then onwards she quickly picked up strength until she was back to her usual form. The reason for her illness remains obscure. I suspect, however, that it may have been due to an over-indulgence in frosted ivy leaves.

Apart from this illness, which might well have resulted in her death, Beauty came through the crucial period of her first winter well. As the first new green shoots of spring became apparent she tried them all, and either rejected them or ate them avidly. Snow-drops and daffodils she decided against, fortunately, but much later when the tulips began to show she ate them down to ground level. We had no tulips in front of our house that spring.

By the end of April the coat change began, from the now shabby and bleached-looking winter coat to the foxy-red thin coat of summer, but it was a full month before the red coat fully replaced the winter one. This coat change occurs with all red deer and it is undoubtedly from the summer coat that the name 'red' deer is taken, for the winter coat is much darker and indeed can look almost black in some lights.

As June came in Beauty was transformed. The ugly patchy appearance of the old winter coat was gone, no doubt to her relief, for it was obvious that she felt very itchy during the transition period, continually pulling patches of loose hair from her coat and rubbing and scratching herself on trees or convenient fence posts. In her new summer coat she looked thinner but sleeker, a really beautiful young hind, foxy red in colour. As new grazing sprang up all around her feeding area, she began to refuse her bottle and when she was a year old I stopped feeding her. For a few days she called, half-heartedly, about the times of her former bottles, but thereafter she settled to a milkless diet. To many people a year on milk may seem a long period, yet I have seen, with the wild deer on the hill, a fifteen- to sixteen-month-old beast sucking on one side of a hind while her three-month-old calf sucked on the other.

Beauty began to lose her milk incisor teeth (that is, the cropping teeth which deer have *only* on their lower jaw, having only a hardened gum-pad on the 'point' of their upper jaw against which these lower incisors cut or pluck) in early June, when about a year old. These milk teeth were lost, at intervals, over a seven-month period, being replaced, one by one, by her permanent incisor teeth until she had a full set of these at nineteen months old. Her molars, that is the 'cudding' teeth on each side of her long jaw which approximate to our back teeth and which are present in upper and lower jaws, took longer, as in wild deer, for she was two and a half years old before the molar milk teeth were all replaced by permanent molars.

When July brought its legions of flies and midges, these winged pests which send the wild deer up to the high ground to find peace, Beauty took refuge in the coolness of the stable during the day, chewing the cud in peace, free from the winged army. Often she varied this by coming into the house, lying on, of all things, a deer-skin rug, in the outer passageway. This, however, we had to stop. Beauty was as far from being house-trained as when she journeyed, lying on my lap, on holiday with us. In her first autumn she had often come right into the house to lie on a more conventional rug in front of our Rayburn stove, with our cat and dog. Happy though we were to have her presence with us indoors, we had to stop this also, for the same reason.

The humid, thunder-in-the-air sultriness of some of the days of high summer made Beauty very restless. If she accompanied me to the hill and I stopped for any length of time, perhaps looking with my 'glass' at distant deer, she would lie beside me for a little, ears constantly flicking and head tossing to shake off the eternal flies, and then suddenly rise and in a short, wild, bucking and cavorting run, seek a peaty, boggy pool or rush-enclosed drain to lie in. Failing this she would lie on a damp, black peat hag. In this she was again following the habit of her wild kindred, who use peat and bogs throughout the year and not just at the rutting time as is widely believed.

30

A rather amusing spectacle presented itself to my eyes towards the end of that summer as I approached home. Down the road from my house fled a Cairn terrier, yelping in fright. Immediately at its rear came Beauty, a front hoof dabbing out at the demoralized terrier. Well behind Beauty toiled an anguished lady, with a figure definitely *not* built for speed, gasping 'shoo, shoo' whenever she could spare breath. Behind her again came the lady's companion who, so far from sympathizing or helping, was doubled up in mirth. Before the chase reached me the terrier had doubled back, enabling the anguished owner to pick it up, whereupon Beauty, instigator of this mad 'frolic', began to graze, a picture of placid-seeming innocence. I am glad to say I was not so unchivalrous as to be doubled up in mirth myself but I will admit I had to struggle to keep my amusement inward instead of outward.

The months went by, until, in September, it was the turn of the thin red summer coat to go, being replaced by the thicker winter coat with its outer guard hairs to shed all the rain and snow that a Highland winter could throw at it, and its invisible inner 'fur', to which neither rain nor snow should penetrate, and which keeps its owner warm in the coldest of the frosts in winter. There were less acorns that autumn but there *was* a bumper crop of rowans. The flavour of these was quite obviously to Beauty's liking for, once discovered, she would not pass a rowan tree until she had satiated herself, even rising erect on her hindlegs to reach berries otherwise too high for her. Her second winter was a much less anxious one for me. Although she was able to find much of her needs in grazing around the house she accepted a little supplementary feeding in the way of potato and apple peelings, cabbage and celery leaves. I found that, while she would not accept corn from my hand, she would watch till she saw me putting a measure of it into the pony's feed-box, so that it could have it when I took it in each evening, and would then go into the stable and steal it. After I found this out I put some in for her daily and then gave the pony its ration when I took it in at night.

A rather peculiar addiction I found she had was for tangerine peel. She excelled herself at Christmas by entering the house while the living-room was empty, and pulling a closed box of tangerines from off the couch. This she managed somehow to get open and when I came in and discovered her there she had a whole tangerine, complete with silver foil, in her mouth. After this incident we saved tangerine peel and my wife, Margaret, put it out on the window sill for her. This led to another amusing incident, for deer have very long memories as far as food is concerned. Margaret also used this same window sill, at times, to put a dish of stewed fruit to cool. One evening we were all at our evening meal when my wife suddenly pushed back her chair and rushed to the window. 'The apples!' she exclaimed. One look at her expression and then at the bare window sill told it all. Sure enough, lying below the window sill outside was the now empty fruit dish. We ate our custard without stewed apples that night.

Curiously enough, though Beauty condescended to enter the stable as a cool refuge on a hot day in summer, or to filch the pony's corn, she would not go into it for shelter on the wildest of winter's nights. She would lie outside enduring with, it appeared, no discomfort, weather which would have us indoors at a warm fire.

I fulfilled, in their Christmas holidays, a promise which my two sons, Lea, then aged nine, and Michael, then aged six, had extracted from me, namely to let them accompany me when I went out with Prince, the pony, to take in a hind. Beauty came too, as did my dogs, so that quite a cavalcade went to the hill that day. I had wondered what Beauty's reaction would be to a dead hind, the first she had seen. It was, in fact, complete indifference; she even had a chew at the hind's ear, thereafter grazing indifferently while I loaded the hind. Accompanying me to the hill to take in deer became a regular occurrence and while doing this she saw many live wild deer and many dead ones. To neither one nor the other did she pay much attention. I was her 'mother', the donor of her milk supply when she was young; wild deer meant nothing to her. The gate to the hill outside my house was always open if she wanted away to the hills and her wild kindred. It was, however, quite evident that she was very content where she was and that was that. There were times when Beauty would let me go to the hill alone, to take in the hinds (which it was my winter's job to stalk, so that the deer's natural yearly increase did not lead to overpopulation, and its consequent evils). More than once, however, when perhaps half way on my return journey with laden pony, Beauty would appear in the distance, nose down to the heather, actually following my scent. That red deer *will* follow a track by scent I already suspected, for I had seen single stags in the rutting period weaving here and there over trackless hill, working out the scent trail left by hinds which had passed ahead of them. Here, however, was confirmation, for my way through the hill was *not* on a fixed path, and yet Beauty had no difficulty in finding me, hours after I had left her lying at home.

By the time she was two years old she had developed a habit of 'investigating' any dog which came within range of her vision, and was completely unafraid of them, large or small. This investigation usually led to an undignified retreat by a demoralized dog while an inquisitively minded hind followed close behind. The most undignified retreat of all was that of a huge deerhound, amazingly so, when one remembers that deerhounds were bred to run down deer. The deerhound was quietly walking past my house, a few yards ahead of its master, when Beauty arrived on the scene, head down, characteristically, sniffing at the deerhound's rump and already drooping tail. Drooping tail drooped still farther, until it was tucked up between the dog's back legs, and its quiet pace quickened to an undignified trot. Beauty also quickened her pace while the man in charge of the deerhound seemed in a quandary as to whether he should attempt to drive Beauty off or to 'buy her off' by stroking her head and making a fuss of her.

Threats and blandishments alike failed utterly, for Beauty waltzed around the man and calmly resumed her inquiry into the nature of this large hairy dog-like creature. The final move in the encounter came when the deerhound broke into an unashamed run and jumped, effortlessly, over an iron gate across the road below my house. Beauty decided the effort of following suit was not worth it and so the chase ended. Admittedly the deerhound, though fully grown, was a young one and had probably never seen a red deer hind before. Nevertheless it was a really diverting sight to watch the 'situation in reverse', a deerhound pursued, and put to flight, by a red deer hind.

In the late May of 1961 I set out early one morning to investigate an eagle's eyrie I knew of, with a single eaglet on it, some ten miles away. I intended to take photographs, if I could, and I did *not* want Beauty's company. She, apparently, took no notice of my unobtrusive (I thought) departure, placidly chewing her cud by the house door. I had hardly gone a mile, congratulating myself that I had escaped her notice, when Beauty caught me up, singling out the path I had gone along from another two possible ones.

33

There was no way of sending her home and so to the eyrie she had to come.

Coming in on a line *above* the eyrie I soundlessly looked over its shielding overhang and saw that the female eagle was on the nest. With the hope of a photograph, at very short range, of the adult eagle I sank back quietly and, with excitement making my fingers all thumbs, I began to set my camera lens. Beauty, however, a law to herself as usual, had different ideas. Having seen my attention momentarily riveted on something below the cliff's edge she too had to see. Ignoring completely my silent but frenzied arm brandishings she trotted forward, right to the cliff edge above the nest, and peered over. She at once started backwards, as if in fright, then insatiable curiosity getting the upper hand she again walked forward and peered over. I can only imagine the astounded and probably outraged eyes of the adult eagle as she transfixed this intruder with that piercing aquiline glare which had caused that initial start back on Beauty's part. A long second elapsed while I silently cursed Beauty, then the eagle flung herself off the eyrie and, getting the wind below her outspread wings, returned low over our heads, even more surprised, I imagine, to find a red deer hind in company with a human. Head bent down, she looked us over well before departing down the long glen, gliding now, as she used the air currents, and soon vanishing from my sight.

While I had nothing left to do but endure my disappointment and make do with the eaglet chick as subject for my camera, Beauty, curiosity evidently assuaged, lay down nearby and began placidly to chew her cud.

I spent some time at the eyrie and, after leaving it, more time in lighting a small wood fire to boil a 'drum' of tea over, before beginning the long return journey. On the way I spied a small group of hinds ahead and decided to try and stalk them in an attempt to secure photographs. Beauty had begun to graze while I had lain motionless working out a possible line of approach, and I had hopes that she might continue while I stalked the hinds. I should have known better! With feminine caprice or simply cervine curiosity she decided she too must have a closer look at the deer. Advancing past my prostrate form, as I snaked slowly closer in the scant cover, she picked a mouthful of grass here and there, eventually arriving at the near fringe of the reclining deer. Despite the commonly voiced belief that deer would smell human scent from a tamed deer and, in consequence, would never accept its proximity, the 'wild' deer, apart from a cursory look as she advanced, took no notice, neither fleeing in fright nor driving off this domesticated relative in anger. As I lay watching, feeling that this fascinating confrontation more than repaid her behaviour at the eyrie, the full implications of the position began to worry me. Could I wriggle back, still unseen, and would Beauty sense my withdrawal and also withdraw, or would she, seemingly content near 'wild' deer, stay with them? Or should I suddenly show myself and would the wild deer run while Beauty, undisturbed by my familiar appearance, remained? I must admit that I just did not know which course she would choose: home with me or home in a different sense with her 'cousins'. While I lay debating, the problem was settled by the sharp eyes of an elderly hind catching a slight movement of mine. Rising to her feet she advanced a little, barked once, and turned to run. Her companions, infected by her alarm, rose and followed her, vanishing over a ridge ahead. Beauty, engrossed in her grazing, paid no heed at all, and when I rose, stretching cramped limbs, in a state of mind between relief and wonder, Beauty followed me home, at times to my rear, at others trotting ahead to graze for a little until I caught her up. The test of whether she preferred the company of her own kind and the wide freedom of their hill-life to my company and the curtailed freedom of a domestic existence had been undergone and she had preferred the latter.

In the autumn of 1961 she was approaching two and a half years old, stood three feet two inches on her cloven hooves, and was nearing the time when young red deer hinds in the Highlands can be expected to feel the first restlessness of the breeding urge. Knowing that this had occasionally occurred with similarly domesticated hinds I had hopes that she might 'take the hill' for herself and, mating urge satisfied, return in due course to have a calf 'at home'. She duly came into season, her restlessness lasting about twenty-four hours, but she seemed to have no inclination to leave the surroundings of the house. Some three weeks later she again came into season, again for twenty-four hours and again stayed at home. Another three weeks elapsed and though it was now late in the year and most of the stags were back in 'bachelor' parties I decided to try and get her to the stags myself. Going out with her in late afternoon I manœuvred her to within fifty yards of a herd of stags, lying, quite undisturbed, chewing their cuds. For long minutes I thought she would spoil it all, for she simply stood above my ground-hugging form, poking at me now and again and snorting through her nostrils. So near were we to the stags that I could not move a muscle; I could only 'will' her to leave me in favour of the stags. At long last this she did, leaving me and going towards the stags who, while I watched, paid no attention whatever to her, in season as she most obviously was. Satisfied, I inched my way out of sight, with visions of Beauty and a calf of her own lying by my house the following June.

The incalculable Beauty had other ideas, however. I can only imagine she must have either ignored, or been ignored by, the recumbent stags and then carried on downhill and jumped the low fence at the roadside below. At all events she arrived at the village of Fort Augustus—as I later heard—that same evening.

I was away from home that evening, at Fort William, and I had hardly started when a phone message, to the effect that Beauty was in the village, was relayed to Margaret. Half an hour later a friend's car arrived, with the same message. It was by then pitch-dark and my wife could do nothing, nor could I when I arrived home near to midnight. No fewer than seven phone messages arrived before half-past eight next morning, telling of the various wanderings of Beauty throughout the village. She had been variously described, by different eye-witnesses, as a donkey and a big, black Alsatian dog. Afterwards, piecing the various reports together, I learnt that Beauty, on the evening of her visit to the village, had visited the British Legion club, accompanying some of the members home across the Caledonian Canal bridge. She had then had a frolic with a Boxer dog, refused various well-intentioned offerings of hand-held bread and later returned back over the canal bridge. In the morning she had visited the Bank of Scotland, the post office and the Lovat Arms hotel. Her last visit on her tour that morning, as reported to me, was to a small primary school at 9 o'clock, to the delight of the children attending it.

When I eventually managed to get to the village at 9.30 I was showered and confused by well-meant advice as to where she had been last seen. After a search of most of the village I found her quietly grazing in the ground of the Benedictine Abbey, much to my relief. She came trotting up to me at once, and then followed me the three miles home, like an outsize dog. Unlike a dog, however, I knew I could not keep her with me if the whim of the moment decided otherwise but fortunately, except when she decided to ford the river which we had to cross, rather than walk across the bridge, she gave me no trouble.

Luckily it had been a winter visit. Had it been summer, with village gardens inviting her to try vegetables and flowers, her popularity with the villagers, to whom she was an attractive novelty, would quickly have waned.

In the following summer, indeed, she blotted her copybook very badly by invading the garden of Culachy Lodge by dint of forcing a small gate sufficiently open for her to squeeze through. While we slept, blissfully unaware of the damage her experimental food-tasting tour of the garden was creating, she cropped and ate to her appetite's content. Gladioli spikes, phlox tops, peas, strawberries, raspberry leaves, all were tried and, as a kind of staple to these, she had walked up and down between rows of cabbage and cauli-flower plants, disdaining their tougher outer leaves but nipping out each young heart as she did so. The strawberries had been netted and here she had contrived to make such a tangle that it was a major task to unravel it. When I discovered her, belatedly, that morning, she was lying, content, replete, and the very picture of placid innocence, on the lawn at the back of the devastated garden and showed extreme reluctance to leave this Paradise discovered, contriving to rip out yet more cabbage hearts before she was blas-phemously evicted.

Once having tasted the illicit sweetness of the garden's produce she became exceedingly difficult to keep out, as is all too typical of the cervine character, whether wild or tame. She contrived to make two more raids, finishing off the surviving gladioli in doing so before the heightened fence and strengthened gate served to keep her out.

A curious insight into the known habit of Highland red deer, of chewing (not eating) strange objects, including carcases of mountain hare, grouse and, on Rhum, shearwaters, was afforded to me in those raids, for Beauty had twice chewed and discarded, as a damp, pulped mess, birds which had been caught in the strawberry net. On another occasion I had seen her chew for minutes a dead mouse, eventually, in this instance also, rejecting the pulped and sodden remains.

It became unwise to leave the house door open even if we were only minutes away on some errand or other. Beauty was now adept at sizing up the situation, perhaps by first peering in the living-room

37

window, and at various times she sampled grapes, bars of milk chocolate (neatly removed from the wrappers), corn which was kept in a jar on the (inside) windowsill for the boys' pet mice, and was once caught in the act, luckily, of pulling an apple tart, plate and all, from off the kitchen table, having discovered nothing to her taste in the living-room.

The polished, shining surfaces of any visitor's car, car-proud or not, were a magnet for Beauty. They were gazed at, prodded at with a moist nose, and breathed on moistly. At times they were licked, an attempt at car-cleaning which left moist streaks on body work or windows and which was seldom appreciated by the car owner. The loud blasting of his horn hurriedly summoned the owner of a motor cycle from the seat by the fire where he had been chatting with me, to find Beauty in the act of again prodding the horn button with an inquisitive nose.

In her last two winters with us Beauty came periodically into season but she never did go and 'search' for a stag, unless that was what took her so often in these periods of unrest to the British Legion club in Fort Augustus. This habit of visiting the village, and her habit of sampling queer items, whether edible or not, may have contributed to her untimely death, for in the January of her fifth year, after I had yet again to go and fetch her from the village late one afternoon, she died, some time in the night.

A character in her own right, self-willed and quite unpredictable as she could be at times, she was also very flattering in that she so often desired to go wherever I went. To no other member of my family, though all had fed her in my occasional absences, would she extend this 'devotion'. At times this 'shadowing' of my foot-steps was neither possible nor welcome but she had acquired an almost Houdini-like ability in forcing open gates, escaping over or through fences and in butting open insecurely closed doors. But while she was an undoubted nuisance at times, the balance was very much on the credit side and her death saddened all of us, even if we were at last freed from wondering what new, undreamt of escapade would have us all in 'hot water' again.

A word of warning for those who may be tempted to keep a 'tame' deer, either red or roe deer. The females of both species can make attractive pets but a hand-reared male, of either species, can be very dangerous. Losing all fear of humans, familiarity engender-ing, if not contempt, an apparent knowledge of their own strength as opposed to man, who is puny indeed without a weapon, fatalities have occurred with humans and tame male deer, involving perhaps the very person who reared them. Irresistible when young, as are so many animals, they can outgrow their welcome just as a cuddlesome puppy can grow into an undesirable dog.

4

Fox Versus Eagle
(*from events partly witnessed, partly deduced*)

THE four cubs toiled wearily in the wake of the big dog fox as he slanted up the steep green face, in the coolness of an early morning in May. Born in late March, they were yet only six weeks old and their short legs and tubby bodies were not designed for long journeys over rough hill ground. To the inexperienced eye they did not look at all fox-like, being still in the soft blue-grey coat of early cubhood. It would be a week or two yet before this coat gradually reddened, beginning with the head, and their bodies lengthened to foxy shape as well as colour.

Only yesterday, there had been five cubs, snugly underground in a cairn-den, in the lower reaches of the glen they had left far below them. Their mother, a young vixen, was curled up asleep in the central chamber of the cairn with around her the five cubs, her first litter. There had burst suddenly in on them a grizzled Cairn terrier, its entry heralded by a scraping of blunt claws on the rocky entrance to the den. The cubs scattered at once into the cracks and crevices which seamed the inside of the cairn but one, nearest to the lunging terrier, was 'snapped' en route and killed instantly by the strong jaws of the terrier. Meanwhile, the rudely awakened vixen, who would normally have been lying outside in cover in the vicinity of the den, but was this time caught inside, had backed into a wide crack in the rock which protected all but her head and her snapping white fangs. To her the terrier bitch now turned her attention. Repeatedly she dashed in, trying for a throat hold on the vixen,

Alert, a red deer hind and her young calf.

A one-antlered stag with six good points. Was his sire a royal or a hummel?

A mature red stag, in velvet, and a two-year-old staggie with only the beginnings of antler growth.

X   A red deer stag, his well-shaped antlers a contrast to the antlerless hinds.

An obviously old hind in poor condition.

Beauty, a dappled beauty indeed, at a fortnight old.

Beauty, still very wobbly-legged, as the author found her.

Beauty and Penny asleep in perfect amity.

Michael and Beauty, firm friends.

Beauty with Penny and two generations of MacNallys, the author's mother and father at back, and his two sons, Michael (left) and Lea (right).

Beauty, planning a clandestine visit to the house, has a preliminary look in the window.

A strange procession wending home through the hill—the author with his dogs, Prince the pony loaded with a dead hind, and Beauty, a very much alive hind.

XVI

Beauty sharing the rug in front of the stove with Penny the springer spaniel.

but unsuccessfully. Once she retreated with blood welling from a punctured snout, while, another time, for minutes the two warring females were locked in a jaw to jaw hold, the terrier's jaws clamped on the slender under-jaw of the vixen while her long fangs were deep in the terrier's nose and upper jaw. Stalemate ensued, the terrier barking and whining but unable to gain a telling hold and the vixen content to stay there and defy her, her cubs safe in narrow cracks into which no terrier could penetrate. The stalker outside, on a routine round of the dens, listened to the tell-tale barking for some time, and later, bending to the mouth of the cairn, smelt the 'turpentine' odour released willy-nilly by the distressed vixen. At length he called his terrier out and, very reluctantly, the bitch eventually obeyed and emerged. The stalker leashed her and waited patiently, gun at the ready, in a commanding position if the vixen should bolt.

Inside the vixen stayed in her position of strength, her lower jaw paining her intensely where the strong teeth of the terrier had punished it. Very gradually in the quiet which now prevailed she relaxed, but soon fear of the terrier's return began to weigh heavily upon her. Here, underground, she was trapped, above ground she could out-distance any terrier and she could also draw it away from the den and her cubs. Suddenly, making up her mind, she quickly made her way up to near the entrance of the cairn. Nothing was visible as she looked, still shielded by the rocks, and all was quiet. Gathering herself, she bolted, a red-furred streak, gaining speed as she reached the open. Fiery needles penetrated her hurtling body, rolling her over, while a loud bang assailed her ears; even as she was conscious of this, blackness overcame her as the stalker administered the *coup de grâce* with his second barrel. Simultaneously, the terrier broke her leash in her frantic struggle to get at the fox and in a moment was worrying at the still red form from which the stalker had to forcibly separate her in order to get her back into the den, to deal with the cubs. In the terrier did go, but the cubs had stayed in their crevices and to the terrier the warm body of the vixen who had so recently punctured her snout held more attraction than a fruitless scraping at immovable rock. She passed a minute or so in worrying the dead cub, the muffled 'gurrying' audible to the listening stalker, and then emerged, trailing the dead cub with her, and nothing would make her go in again. The stalker, satisfied on the evidence of dead vixen and cub that the den had been dealt with, left the dead vixen at the den's entrance and went on to check one or two more dens before turning for home. He did consider waiting all night at the den, in case the dog fox should come in, but with the desirability of completing his round uppermost in his mind, he carried on, a lucky decision for the surviving cubs.

The dog fox had had a long night's hunting and had at last been lucky enough to kill a rabbit as it nibbled grass near the high ground warren where a small colony of hill-rabbits had escaped the vile scourge of myxomatosis which had almost wiped out their lower ground brethren. Knowing nothing of the very young rabbits left by the dead doe dangling from his jaws, now doomed to starvation, the dog fox approached the den shortly before dawn and was immediately alerted by the taint of man and terrier which still clung around it. Noiselessly putting down the rabbit he hastily scooped some moss over it and, slinking slowly forward, went around the den in a wide and wary circle, sensitive ears cocked and even more sensitive nose testing the air ceaselessly. Working ever closer to the den he caught the body scent of the dead vixen and relaxed for a moment. But something was wrong. Why did she not come to meet him to relieve him of the prey he would surely have? An old and vigilant dog who owed his longevity to the keenness of his senses, he had lost more than one vixen under somewhat similar conditions and now, as he slunk closer to the den, he knew he had lost another. Sniffing at the dead vixen, his long snout wrinkled in an expressive snarl as he smelled man and terrier scent also. Into the den he went and through to the central chamber. At the slight sounds of his arrival the cubs, their senses alerted by the increasing chilliness of their separate crevices, waited warily, but then, catching his familiar scent, came tumbling to meet him. The scent of the terrier was still unpleasantly strong inside the den to the dog fox, and he wasted no time but turned and led out of the den, the cubs following as if at some inaudible command.

The dog led the small procession straight to the rabbit as if aware of their need for nourishment for the journey ahead and stood by impatiently while they fought over it, the strongest getting the major share until there was little left. Normally, full-bellied now, the cubs would have slept but the dog fox, on edge because of the den's destruction and knowing full well of the imminence of daylight in which he did not care to travel overmuch, somehow communicated to them the necessity of following him, and led off towards a cairn he knew, on the remote high ground where he had denned with impunity in former years. Even as they now approached it he was uneasy; it was now full daylight and he felt very exposed on the high green ridge, just on the other side of which lay the small cairn, a jumble of grey slabs in a shallow gully in the bottom of which ran a little burn, a necessity in providing water near to the den for the needs of the cubs. Topping the ridge he viewed with relief the cairn just below. Towards it he went quickly, eager to have its shelter, and one, two and three of the cubs followed him over. The fourth, the runt of the litter, had lost some ground in the last steep climb and was now some way behind, but put on a valiant spurt as he saw the last cub vanish over the ridge.

To the male eagle, high above, he was little more than a speck worth investigating, for he too had young to feed, a single eaglet on an eyrie further up the long glen. He went into a shallow but incredibly fast glide, wings held stiffly and half closed and quickly bore down on the cub. The cub, sensing in the last seconds of his life the huge black shape nearly on top of him, mustered up despairing strength in a last race forward, a futile race which ended in a faint squeal as the breath was forced from his body in the clutch of one huge, steel-taloned foot. Balancing for an instant on one foot, the other slightly outstretched ahead of him clutching the dead cub, the eagle glanced haughtily around with cold and imperious eye, then flung itself off the ridge and, gaining height, flew to its eyrie, the small limp form dangling from one foot.

Under cover in the den the dog did not really comprehend that he had lost one cub. He had three around him in the cairn and that satisfied his parental instinct, and they were all well away from the dangerous proximity of the discovered den.

For a fortnight thereafter they had fared well enough. The dog fox had killed the only lamb out on that high ground, that of a blackface ewe which had been unwise enough to stray out there while all the other sheep were still on the lower ground, and he had had a grouse hen or two, and their eggs. By a lucky accident he had almost stumbled over a hen ptarmigan as she sat tight on eight hard-set eggs and this too went to feed his hungry cubs. Towards the end of May he had another lucky break in finding a dead deer calf, one which had died shortly after birth, on a small green beside the burn in the coire's bottom. This calf, heavier than average, weighed eighteen and a half pounds, and the fox 'cut' it expertly in two, midway along the spine, carrying first one half and then the other into the den. The last few days had been rather lean, however, lean as the fox himself in his constant foraging; a few voles or so, a dead hoodie left below its shattered nest by a stalker, and an occasional nest full of half-fledged meadow pipits hardly sufficing to blunt the cubs' growing appetites. So it was that the fox, coming cautiously, a red shadow, up a green ridge above the den, halted quickly and sank to a jaw-drooling crouch beside a huge grey rock.

They made a charming picture in the strengthening light of the June dawning, the daintily dappled deer calf, only hours old, and the fond mother, patiently submitting to its greedy sucking. To the lurking watcher, however, they meant only one thing: food. The big fox, hungry himself, had hungry cubs to feed and deer calf would satisfy their appetites for a day or two.

Tempting though the sight was, the fox knew better than to risk the sharp, lashing hoof-strokes of the hind's plunging forefeet, having had painful experience of this in his impetuous youth, and so he lay low and waited. Its feed finished, the infant calf was sleepy and only too willing to subside onto the grassy floor of the high green coire where it had lately been born. The mother, after grazing desultorily nearby for a short while, moved away slowly, picking a mouthful as she went. To a chance onlooker now, she was only a single hind grazing in the coire, but the red watcher knew better. He watched the hind go and half rose once or twice as if to dart across to the unsuspecting calf, but each time, judgment overruling eagerness, he subsided beside his rock again.

At last the hind topped the ridge above and disappeared out of sight. Another few minutes elapsed and then the fox could wait no longer—a red flash across the green of the coire, a muffled, bewildered half-bleat from the rudely awakened calf as the long fangs pierced its neck and it was all over. The dog fox had been returning to his den with only a barely fledged wheatear as prey, prey which he had caught as it fluttered up from his feet, but here now was a lucky windfall indeed. The calf had been born only a quarter of a mile or so from the rocky cairn which held the cubs and slightly uphill from it, and so, though an entire red deer calf is heavy prey for a hill fox, he did not wait to 'cut' it in two but half dragged, half lifted it down the short distance to the den. Now and again he almost tripped as the long legs of the calf tangled up with his own, but he kept going as fast as he could, fearful of the pounding of hooves behind him, signifying the return of the hind. She, however, was peacefully grazing, by now nearly a mile away, building up nourishment to convert into milk for a calf which would need it no longer.

Arriving at last at the den, the weary fox pulled the limp carcase to near the shelter of a huge slab and at once, in a concerted rush, three furry bodies were snarling and tugging at it. Their juvenile snarls were comical in cubs so young, but nevertheless menacing enough to themselves as each jealously warned off the other.

The den, tenanted for some weeks now, was becoming increasingly foul. In among its rocks were strewn the shoulder blades, pelvic bones, rib girdle and lower legs of the previous deer calf, not a shred of flesh on the bones. A little way off, in the bottom of the gully, where the cubs had been playing foxy football with them, lay the calf's head, cheek by jowl with that of the blackface lamb, with, nearby, a scattering of wool and two black forelegs. Paths were trodden to and from the water, droppings were scattered about and holes had been scraped here and there, exposing black peat below the green as the cubs' growing restlessness and digging instincts asserted themselves. Inside the den the stench was fearful to the human nose, but apparently meant nothing to the foxes, who amid all the stench and foulness kept their coats scrupulously clean, with a glossy sheen on them.

And so it was that when a few days later a shepherd on one of the annual sheep gatherings came to the top overlooking the cairn his experienced eye told him at once that there was a den. His face a little grim when he noted the lamb remains, he did not go near the den, but calling his dogs quietly he gave it a wide berth. On his arrival home he at once told the estate stalker.

About 8.30 that evening, the estate stalker, reinforced by two colleagues from neighbouring estates, approached the den quietly keeping their eager terriers in check, hoping at that hour in the evening to get a shot at vixen or dog, or even at cubs venturing impatiently outside the den while waiting hungrily for the arrival of the dog fox with prey. A cub was seen in fact, but it darted in so quickly that not a shot was fired. The terriers, unmanageable now that a fresh fox scent was blowing direct to them from the den, darted forward and into the cairn. Inside, this small cairn was not nearly as impregnable as the one in which the cubs had been born, and the cubs were now larger, so that to the accompaniment of whines, barks and the scrabbling of claws on rock, the three cubs, one by one, spitting and snarling to the last, were killed by the terriers. Listening to the dogs working inside, the stalkers had time to look around the cairn and they were more angered by the pitiful remains of the deer calves than at the lamb remains. Twice during their wait a terrier backed out, dragging a dead cub and later, when all had emerged, the third cub was fished out with a long stick from where it was dimly visible in a deep fissure in the cairn.

The cubs having been dealt with, the stalkers decided to wait out all night in case the vixen or dog fox should appear. In the tardy gloaming of the short summer night one stalker glimpsed a shadow drift silently across the gully, to the east of the den, well out of range of his gun, and he rose quietly and hurried over the opposite ridge in the slender hope of catching the fox if it came sneaking round for a look from that ridge top. The fox, however, arrived at the ridge top long before the hurrying stalker and took in the situation at a glance, before fading away, silently. Shortly after this, deer began to feed in, skylined on the ridges until each had its frieze of grazing deer, on their way down into the glen for their night's grazing. In marked contrast to the sedate pace downwards of the grazing hinds, single hinds were coming in at intervals, some so keen as to be literally galloping down into the coire, eager to rejoin calves left lying there when they were disturbed by the sheep-gathering that day. While yet there was sufficient light (and it was only between 2 and 3 a.m. that it was truly dark) one of the stalkers watched a hind, bleached-looking in old winter coat, 'pick up' a dappled calf about half a mile west of the den, very close to the line they had taken in approaching the cairn. The calf ran to meet the mother as she came near and began to suck greedily, small tail wagging furiously in ecstasy, while the hind, head bent round, licked assiduously at its dappled form, cherishing her young one. Later, she led off slowly down into the coire where she would stay, grazing, with her calf all of the short night, working out again in the early hours of the morning, leaving the calf to lie alone once more whenever it grew tired of following her.

An orange-red sunset gave way to a three-quarter moon, and the night grew colder, though not unpleasantly so. Snipe were bleating late and recommenced early again. A golden plover called plaintively shortly after midnight, seeing the slinking dog fox as he crouched to windward of the den, nose wrinkled in distaste at the scent of men and dogs. All throughout the night a cock ptarmigan, apparently sharing the vigil, croaked gutturally from the rocky face opposite

46

the cairn. With the coming of the red dawning, heralded by the voice of a cuckoo far below in the wooded river banks, the stalkers redoubled their vigilance, but except for the ptarmigan still on guttural guard, they saw nothing. Conscious that at least there would be no more killing to feed hungry cubs, they gave it up at last and 'brewed up' some hot sweet tea over a fire of heather stalks. The ridges about the den were bright with sunlight as they left, yet, below them, to around the 2,000 feet level, everything was hidden under a white woolly mist, reflecting back the bright rays of the sun, and seeming of the consistency of cotton wool. Upon this woolly 'screen' the sun's beams projected the figures of the three stalkers, dark shadowy shapes, surrounded by a nimbus of rainbow hue, until they disappeared into the mist.

The dog fox watched them go, indeed followed them for a bit, before returning cannily to the den and testing the early morning's light airs to make doubly sure all was safe. At the den his nose and eyes told him the whole story. A moment he sniffed at the three dead cubs, then he turned and vanished over the ridge top to where he had cached a young blue hare, caught the night before. From now on he had only himself to hunt for.

A little later that morning the eagle glided on patrol high above the den ridge as had been his wont since the fox family had taken up residence. Deprived by the cubs' alertness of a live capture he now availed himself of their death, carrying the limp forms one by one to the hungry eaglet, a mile distant as the eagle flew.

The estate stalker, checking up quietly on the den early next day in case he got a chance at an adult fox, was at first nonplussed when he found the cubs gone, but suddenly remembering the eyrie further up the glen, went there, to have his suspicions confirmed by seeing the part-eaten carcase of the last of the cubs lying on the eyrie beside the almost fully fledged eaglet. And so, he reflected briefly as he left for home, the cubs, nourished by the deaths of the young of many species, had only served, in the end, to nourish the young of yet another species, in that busy, relentless time of year when all wildlife strives to ensure the propagation of *their* species, and survival truly goes to the fittest—and luckiest.

5

Dainty, the Roe Who Renounced Her Freedom

THE void left in the family by the premature death of Beauty, the red deer hind who had enriched our lives at Culachy even when at her most infuriating, was filled a little more than two years later with the arrival of a roe deer fawn on a day in late June. I must confess to a certain reluctance in giving names to creatures of the wild, my 'pet' detestation being the name of 'Bambi' bestowed on innumerable young deer since the film of that title captured the public imagination. Nevertheless an animal so constantly with us could hardly remain anonymous and there was no problem in deciding on a name for the tiny roe doe. Dainty was the obvious and quite irresistible name for her, a name which was as appropriate for her when she was fully adult as when she was only days old.

Roe deer are of course very much smaller than red deer and, unlike red deer which of necessity have had to take to the bare high ground in the more remote areas of Scotland, roe are seldom far from the cover of woodlands and their associated undergrowth. They are widespread throughout Scotland and throughout most of England (there is one rather puzzling 'blank spot' in the Midlands of England), but in Ireland, more puzzling still perhaps, there are *no* roe deer.

Dainty weighed only 4 lb. 6 oz. within a day or two of her birth, whereas a red deer calf will average 14–15 lb. at birth, a very considerable difference.

Because of this small size, and also because they seem very much

48

shyer and more sensitive than red deer, roe deer are much more difficult to hand rear, and for all of an anxious first week I had difficulty in getting Dainty to accept milk from a bottle. Whereas Beauty, after the first day or so of strangeness, became thereafter 'greedy' for her bottle, charging towards me when I appeared at each feeding-time, Dainty had to be coaxed out, particularly in that interminable first week. She accepted cow's milk eventually, however, getting it fresh as we did from the farm nearby, taking a thrice-daily ration of 6½ oz. initially, stepped up to 8½ oz. three times a day as she grew older. She was also quicker to sample greenstuffs than Beauty had been, trying grass before she was a week old and supplementing her milk with grass and other greenstuffs increasingly from thenceforward.

In appearance she was a 'sandier' red of coat than a red deer calf with her dapples more irregularly disposed, merging on each shoulder blade, in fact, into a ragged splotch of yellow-white. She was infinitely daintier (it is almost impossible to describe roe deer without recourse to the word 'dainty') than a red deer calf, indeed she appeared fragile with her thin but steel-strong legs terminating in their tiny, pointed black-lacquered hooves.

It was instructive to note, almost from birth, how the habits of these two species of deer native to Britain differed. Beauty, the red deer calf, had lain out quite openly in her grass yard. Dainty was *never* seen when at rest, she was always among or behind the patches of nettles left as cover around the perimeter of her enclosure. Ever on the alert, and obviously tensed up at anything and everything unfamiliar, her tiny red tongue would flick out over her jetty-black nose whenever she was really nervous, a habit she retained even when adult, as do 'wild' roe deer also. This is not entirely simply a 'nervous' habit, but perhaps, conscious or not, partly an attempt to 'sharpen-up', by moistening, the already keen powers of scent which roe and red deer alike possess. For exercise, in her first few weeks, when she was confined mainly to her yard, she would dash madly about in her own beaten-out figure-of-eight running track, a track eventually worn deep into the grass of the enclosure.

Like Beauty, and for the same reasons, Dainty was reared among my terriers and she grew up without fear of them, but she never attempted nor attained the complete ascendancy of Beauty in chasing them about or in stealing their dog biscuits. Nor would she ever willingly enter house or stable, having an evident antipathy to entering into 'the unknown' of enclosed premises.

Her dappled coat, never as distinctly marked as in red deer, lost its juvenile dapples shortly after Dainty was a month old, a few, about her haunches, only remaining and these were only faintly seen markings on her red-brown coat. Besides grazing, Dainty now enjoyed browsing on any tree leaves within her reach, particularly relishing those of wild cherry, ash, rowan, and silver birch.

As with Beauty, there came the problem of what to do with Dainty when we went on holiday. Luckily, my brother Hugh still lived only twelve miles away and was quite prepared to have Dainty while we went away for a week. I assumed, too hastily as it transpired, that Dainty would accept transport by Land Rover as readily as Beauty had done. Had I given it a bit more thought I would have realized that Dainty's more 'highly strung' nature and her reluctance to enter even the enclosed space of our house did not augur well for a placid acceptance of journey by Land Rover. The journey in fact turned out to be a positive nightmare for me, so obviously and progressively did Dainty become distressed, refusing to rest on my lap, refusing even the tranquillizer of her bottle, not only on the journey over, but also on the day following. The return journey a week later was even worse; I could actually *feel* the stress-induced quickened thumping of her heart as I carried her from the Land Rover to her yard, and it was a full week before she was entirely recovered from the effects of the double journey.

By October of her first year she was truly immaculate—there is just no other word for it—in her first sleek and yet thick winter coat. As Beauty had, so also Dainty had, complete freedom to wander around the house and to go to the hill behind, but unlike Beauty she was always nervy of anyone or anything strange and in particular she detested strange dogs, once clearing a six-foot-high gate when alarmed by a shepherd's collie.

Their first winter with its chills and frosts is always a testing time for young deer, whether red or roe, more so for hand-reared deer whose grazing may be limited, so that, denied free ranging to frost-free grazing they may eat more of frosted grazing than is good for them. I had almost lost my red deer calf, Beauty, in her first winter due, I believe, to this, and Dainty too fell sick in her first winter, the usual first indication, refusal of her bottle, warning me of this. Unwilling though she was, Dainty was carried into the warmth of the house, where she lay lethargically by my chair, refusing, for two days, all milk-feeds. At times she would rise to her feet, obviously suffering severe stomach pains, kicking out spasmodically with her hindlegs and nuzzling and prodding at her flanks with her black-tipped muzzle. Though she would take no milk I was able to coax her to eat fresh and fortunately still green leaves of raspberry and brambles. Little of these as she ate, nosing fastidiously at each leaf before slowly chewing or rejecting it, it was sufficient to keep her alive until she recovered from her upset. Just before the end of that year Dainty again refused her milk, this time for good; in other words, she weaned herself at about six months old, another difference between red and roe deer, for Beauty continued to look and call for milk until she was a year old.

The coming of spring and the growth of new greens all around us was welcome indeed when it arrived. Dainty *had* survived and from now on was busily experimenting with the exciting new and fresh scents and tastes of leafage and flower arising on every hand. In the wealth of 'green bites' around the house it was unnecessary for Dainty to forage far afield and the gate to the hill was kept shut. Shut or not, Dainty disappeared one morning and did not reappear until evening, neither her departure nor her return being actually witnessed. How or where had she got out and returned—by squeezing through fence wires or by jumping fence or gate? Try as hard as I did I could not see her at this vanishing act, though she continued to disappear and reappear at will. And then one day, still scratching my head about it, I noticed a few wiry hairs from Dainty's loosening old winter coat caught *under* the bottom bar of the iron gate. Given this clue I then watched until the almost incredible sight of Dainty squeezing through between the rigid iron bar at the bottom of the gate and the equally rigid hard earth confirmed what the hairs first afforded evidence of, unwilling as I was to believe it. The actual space between the bottom bar of that gate and the ground below I measured later and found that it was just ten inches at its maximum. No wonder that roe deer could appear as if by magic *inside* tightly deer-fenced plantations in the Highlands, vulnerable as many of these are with loose, ill-fitting wooden 'water-gates', where their fences cross the ever-present hill-burns or drains. In considering deer, even roe deer, small as they are, few people would think of securing a gap of only ten inches at the bottom of a netting fence. Profiting, however, by having seen for myself Dainty doing her creeping act under the gate, I have since found evidence that wild roe deer are just as expert at 'creeping' through tiny, unregarded gaps as was Dainty. A hole or entrance below a netting fence which will take say, a badger, will also take a roe if it is intent on getting to the other side of the apparently impenetrable barrier.

Knowing that 'tame' hinds in other parts of the Highlands had gone 'temporarily' to the hill, restless with their mating urge, and, unrest quenched in their successful finding of a stag, had subsequently returned home to have a calf in due course, I had always hoped that my own tame hind Beauty would do likewise. For some strange reason known only to herself, however, in Beauty's periods of mating unrest she had always gone down into the village of Fort Augustus, intriguing and usually delighting those of the village folk who saw her but doing herself no good whatever. Dainty, however, in her very first year as a young doe did better. She disappeared to the birch woods that fringed the hill ground at Culachy in late July (mid-July to mid-August being the rutting-time of the roe deer) and day followed day without her reappearance 'home'. At first I was not unduly anxious; her unrest assuaged, she would surely return about the end of August. Her non-appearance then was first fretted-at and then, willy-nilly, accepted with 'of course there is plenty to eat out in the woods just now'. The lean periods of autumn and winter followed with still no reappearance of Dainty, despite my last forlorn hope that winter's hard weather would send her home. I became unwillingly reconciled to the unpalatable fact that Dainty had gone back to her wild kindred for good. This at least was preferable, if less flattering, to the human who had reared her, than the thought that she had met an untimely death in a 'wild' world fraught with perils unknown in her artificial upbringing. Heavy snowfall in November ushered in a long, hard winter and though I kept my eyes peeled, as indeed I had to, in the almost daily jaunts I had to the white hills while hind-stalking, not a sign of Dainty did I ever see.

Spring arrived again, welcome as usual after the long winter. Still no sign of Dainty nor any hint as to her continued existence. I had by now accepted the fact that she was *not* going to return but how welcome even the occasional sight of her, warily keeping her distance, would have been.

In May I went to a meeting in Dumfriesshire of the British Deer Society, and returned home in the early hours of a never-to-be-forgotten morning to find my wife still waiting up for me, all smiles and full of undisclosed glad news. Though it was into the small hours of the morning, being near to 3 a.m., our boys, Lea and Michael, had been striving to keep awake, though up in bed, to tell me themselves of Dainty's return. They had noticed her from their bedroom window about 7 a.m. the previous morning, grazing unconcernedly in the grassy yard behind the house, after arriving as, nay, more unexpectedly than, she had departed. This back yard had a secure gate to it usually left open at nights, and it was only the work of minutes for the excited boys to rush down and shut it with Dainty secure and evidently content inside. Though I was more than ready for my bed I could not possibly go without first seeing how Dainty was and out I went to find that, unbelievably, she was as tame as when she had left us, and came to me at once to eat some titbits from my hand.

I went to bed that early morning in May, my mind churning over with excited speculation. The utterly incredible had happened. An animal which had been 'back to the wild' for almost the length of a year had chosen, voluntarily, to return. There could surely only be one explanation, one instinct strong enough to explain this. Dainty had come back to where she had herself been reared to have, in turn, her fawn. And so indeed it proved, for about three weeks later, on 13th June to be exact, at about seven in the morning, Dainty had her first fawn, a male, in the scanty cover of some young nettles. It weighed almost the same as she had at a similar period in life, about 4 lb. 6 oz., and was a delicate, damp-looking, wee creature, standing on very shaky legs, legs which folded up under it as Dainty licked and washed the sticky dampness of birth from its coat, before lying down beside it and allowing its exploring muzzle to find her udder for its first feed. This, in itself, was new to me, for used to red deer as I was, I had never seen red deer give suck, or allow their recumbent calves to suck, whilst lying down. Indeed I had instead lain and watched hinds assiduously lick and clean their new-born calves for about half an hour after birth, by which time these calves, after several abortive attempts would be standing, tottery-legged, it may be, and attempting to find the udder as the hind stood over their shaky tininess. For the first few feeds of its life then, Dainty allowed her fawn to suckle while both lay down. After the first two days, however, the fawn invariably fed standing from its also standing mother.

Being confident now that the 'pull' of her fawn would bring

Dainty back, even if allowed full freedom 'out the back', I began again to let her have the fuller freedom of around the house and out to the birch woods beyond. In feeding an increasingly lusty fawn Dainty needed to forage more widely than when only feeding herself, and this she was free to do. Noting how Dainty fed her fawn made me look back, wryly, at my insistence on the regularity of the thrice-daily bottle while hand-rearing Dainty. None of that artificial human nonsense for Dainty. She quite often left the fawn for twelve to sixteen hours without feeding and indeed, in the third week in July (the mating season again), she was away for all of thirty-six increasingly anxious hours, while her five-week-old fawn got by on green-stuff alone, rejecting strongly any attempt at bottle-feeding it with milk. Whenever Dainty did return, whether after an absence of twelve or thirty-six hours, she would give a little, almost inaudible (to human ears) wheezy squeak, the doe's call to her young, and this she would repeat until let through the closed gate to where her fawn was waiting expectantly for her and its feed of milk. Dainty was a tender mother even if she did spend a considerable time away from her offspring. After feeding, which only occupied a few minutes, she would spend another few minutes licking and nuzzling her fawn while it nuzzled and nudged at her in return, much enjoyment being apparently derived by both in this reciprocal caressing.

At other times, after feeding had renewed its energies, the fawn would race madly around the grassy yard, brimming over un-controllably with the joy of living, bucking, twisting, dancing, flinging its heels in the air, while Dainty, infected with like abandon, bucked and cavorted with him. Even this early in life, too, the young male fawn's instinct to butt with his tiny head, antlerless as it was, was strong, for as part of that same abandoned play he would often lower his head and butt playfully at Dainty's flanks. As a conse-quence of this 'dancing display' as a fawn, we eventually christened Dainty's first fawn Dance.

In pointed contrast to this wild abandon when Dainty was with him, Dance, in her absence, particularly in the first month of his life, was never to be seen in the open during the day, lying in the cover of the long grass or nettles which fringed his yard, a good pointer to the habits of roe in the wild.

Another very pointed contrast, in view of Dainty's tameness and willingness to submit to and enjoy a gentle scratching behind the ears, was the complete and utter refusal of the 'mother-reared' (as distinct from 'bottle-reared' even though as frequently in contact with humans) fawn to submit to any human handling at all. This suited me, for let me repeat the warning I have already given: 'hand-reared' male deer can be deadly dangerous after they reach the antlered stage, for there are plenty of cases on record, including some personally known to me, of red deer stag or roe buck attacking with the utmost vindictiveness the human beings with whom their utter familiarity has bred, it is quite evident, a knowledge of their helplessness when without a weapon in their hands. Nor does the fact that the human concerned may have been personally responsible for their survival and for the daily milk feeds necessary in extreme youth seem to matter. In fact I must unwillingly admit that male deer, whether red or roe, seem quite incapable of affection as we know it. With hind or doe it appears to be a different matter; after years of experience with, first, Beauty my red deer hind, then with Dainty, I am convinced that the females *can* feel affection for the human who has reared and hand-fed them. This affection, however, is like that of a cat, rather than the unquestioning devotion vouchsafed by a dog for its master or mistress, being shown only when the hind or doe feels like it and being largely forgotten when their still essentially wild nature decrees otherwise. The lack of affection in male deer is more easily understood when one realizes that their world, after they attain maturity, is that of trial by strength, from 'winning' the best feeding to the climax of their year, the winning and retaining by brute force of the females in the rutting season. The females on the other hand do at least feel maternal affection all their lives, the devotion of deer to their young being such that a situation absolutely fraught with perils, such as the presence of a dreaded human, may be utterly ignored in the strength and unthinking devotion of the mother's feelings.

I have had both roe deer and red deer mothers circle around me closely, while I have been kneeling to photograph a discovered young one, my presence being unmistakable to them both by sight and by scent; this presence of man, which is at other times shunned like the plague, being dared in their selflessness.

By the end of his first November Dance had little hair-covered knobs visible on his head, the first sign of the antlers he would later grow. By then, too, at the age of about five months, Dance was being weaned, for Dainty became increasingly reluctant to allow him to suck, eventually refusing altogether.

Although male roe deer share with male red deer the annual casting and subsequent regrowth of antlers, the time of year when they do this is utterly different from that of red deer. The necessity or reason for this casting and regrowth of antlers is still not understood. Antlers, in male deer, are definitely used as defensive weapons and, perhaps more particularly in roe deer, as offensive weapons, in contesting the right to territory or coveted females at the mating times. Yet, in the case of roe, the males are annually left antlerless for an approximate period from late November to early March (in mature bucks) and, in red deer, the stags are antlerless from late March until early August, when once again they are seen cleaning the velvet from off their regrown antlers. The puzzle of actual antler-casting and regrowth is bad enough without its being further complicated by two species, both indigenous to Britain and both of which exist in similar habitat, having different antler-casting periods. It may be argued that red deer are deer of the bare hill and roe deer are deer of woodland and undergrowth, as indeed they are in the Highlands of Scotland nowadays. It should be remembered, however, that red deer too were originally of woodland habitat and have been driven by sheer necessity for survival to the bare hills. Even so there are many areas of Highland Scotland where the two species overlap and in a sense share habitats. It is no uncommon sight at the height of summer to see roe out on the heather hills some distance from woodland nor is it by any means unusual to see red deer in woodland adjacent to hill ground, particularly in winter. We do know that antler-growth is closely related to hormones possessed by male deer and so related in some measure to their breeding times. One reason for the different casting-times in these two species sharing similar climate and habitat is probably that roe deer have their mating time from mid-July to mid-August whereas red deer rut from late September until late October. Roe deer antlers are cast approximately three and a half months after the height of male hormone activity at their rut, and red deer antlers are cast approximately four to five months after the height of their breeding activity. Why they are cast (leaving their former owners defenceless for a period annually, and regrown again) remains a matter for conjecture. And *why* the different mating-times anyway?

To get back to Dance, however, his first 'knobs' were unmistakably conical in appearance, each one coming to a distinct point of hair, and were about an inch long. At this stage they re-

Curled up asleep, brush
wrapped warmly around it.

A pine marten at the
entrance to its den.

Close up of a fox cub.

The hill fox has developed
a genius for seeing while
remaining unseen.

The terrier was more in-
terested in the still-warm
vixen.

The dog fox with rabbit as prey for his cubs.

The turned-out skin of a fox cub lying on an eyrie.

A fox alert outside his den.

XXII

Fox cubs eagerly awaiting the parent's return with food.

Feeding time for a young red deer calf.

XXIV

mained until the beginning of February when the point of hair terminating each 'knob' was replaced by a small tip of yellow-brown bone (the 'button-stage' in young roe bucks). These 'buttons' Dance retained for almost three weeks only, both of them being cast by 17th February. It was only *after* this, being first apparent on 22nd February, that the real growth of Dance's first antlers began and by 1st March he had elongated knobs over an inch in length. By 1st April he had three and a half inches of velvet-covered antlers on each side and by 12th April he had antlers of about six inches in length, with short points, three on one side, two on the other, encased still in grey velvet but quite hard to the touch. He was indulging increasingly in rough butting-play with Dainty, stabbing at her flanks and soft underparts, at times throwing her bodily aside in the vigour of his mock-warfare. At 6 a.m. on 9th May of the year following his birth Dance had one antler 'clean' of velvet and was vigorously rubbing his antlers up and down a sapling with a trunk of about an inch in diameter, removing bark from the sapling and velvet from his antlers with an audible harsh scraping sound. He was at this vigorous 'fraying' for most of the 9th, at times pausing to nibble at the fraying stock, wandering off to graze, then returning, with renewed vigour, to the task of removing the velvet from his first antlers, a task he only finally completed by midday on the 10th May.

On 17th June, while I was out on the hill, Dainty gave birth to twins, both males weighing each about 4 lb. She had her two fawns lying, separately hidden from birth, in the long grass and nettles which bordered the yard I had them in and she herself lay apart from them except when feeding them. Wise dispensation of Nature as this undoubtedly was (ensuring probable survival for one of the twins should the other be discovered by a fox or eagle hunting for food to feed its own young, instead of death for them both), it completely shattered the popular mind's eye picture of mother and infant roe all lying cosily and 'picturesquely' together. As they grew older, however, and more capable of evading any predator by fleet-ness of foot, the twins began to lie together and with Dainty, when she returned from her excursions to the hill, resumed now that she again had the tie of young to ensure her return.

And so the pattern of Dainty's semi-domesticated life continued, most of her summers being spent 'in the wild', while she came 'home' every evening to attend to her fawns, while her winters were spent in the bigger area of enclosed grass and bushes behind my house, the grass of the kennel yard being insufficient in the lean days of each winter to support the roe. On occasion, when it suited her own capricious nature, Dainty accompanied us on our summer picnics but usually she had other business on hand, electing to go to the hill alone instead of with us.

In 1968 she was 'yeld', that is, she had no fawn in that year, but in 1969, the year I left Culachy, she had a fawn, again a male, on 8th June, about midday. I missed the actual birth by about half an hour; Dainty was still industriously cleaning and licking the damp-coated fawn when I arrived on the scene.

The question of having to transport Dainty and her offspring to Torridon, where I had already arranged to have an enclosure for them, was now looming large in my mind. I was not looking forward to it at all, remembering the state of stress she had been in as a fawn, on a journey of only twelve miles. How would she react on a very much longer journey, of about ninety miles, to Torridon? I had a crate made so that Dainty and her new fawn could travel in that together, and also one each for the two bucks I had retained from her previous offspring, Dance and Dash. I had originally intended only to take Dance with Dainty and her new fawn, but arrangements for a friend to take the other buck fell through at the last moment and both bucks had to go. Neither buck was anything like as tame as Dainty, for whereas she would allow, indeed obviously enjoyed, a leisurely scratch behind head and ears, neither of the others, though reared with humans constantly in sight or earshot, would allow human hand to touch them. It was in fact a major operation involving the help of quite a few friends, as well as Lea and Michael, to get the two bucks into their travelling crates. I had been giving them a daily ration of grain, at first by the open end of their crates, gradually leaving it farther and farther inside their crates so that eventually they were entering them quite readily. On the day of the move, with Dainty already safely crated and under the effects of a tranquillizer, we got Dash, the younger buck, crated easily, waiting till he was right inside his crate before creeping quietly up and letting down the sliding door behind him. Dance was a tougher proposition, however, and we made many abortive attempts before we had him similarly crated. Near to despair and exhaustion at last, after Dance had eluded us in last-minute evasive tactics time after time as we were within an ace of shutting him in, Michael conceived the idea of rigging up a long-distance control for the sliding door so that it could be operated from a window of the house. A weird-looking contrivance of much-knotted string and wire was rigged up and, weird-looking or not, it worked and we had Dance captive at last. Both bucks were tranquillized as Dainty had been, and all travelled without mishap over the long miles to Torridon, where, the effects of the tranquillizing injections having worn off, they were glad to bound out of their narrowly confined quarters to the grass of their new enclosure. The only casualty as a result of the upset of the long journey and completely new and strange 'habitat' was the new fawn. Only three weeks old, the stress must have been too much for it, though this was not apparent until, going out two mornings after our transfer, I found its small dappled form stiff and cold. The others settled well after a period of initial strangeness. The main difficulty at Torridon has been the relative scarcity of deciduous trees as compared to Culachy. In rearing the roe I had early recognized the importance of 'browse' in their dietary requirements, particularly in winter, for grass alone was quite evidently not enough for a wood-land species. I had therefore made a practice of regularly bringing in bunches of browse for the roe, wild cherry, ash, rowan, oak and elm, while the leaves of these were available, and ivy mainly, throughout the leafless winters. However, we 'made do', and luckily, through the kindness of a new neighbour, we had the whole of a luxuriantly grown ivy-covered wall to keep us going in winter with its evergreen leaves.

Dainty is seven years old as I write this and as tame and delightful as ever without as yet any evident signs of old age. Ten to twelve years of age is about the maximum for 'wild' roe in the Highlands so, I hope, we still have some years of the pleasure of Dainty's presence left.

She has no fawn this year (1971) but a wild goat kid which I reared on the bottle has adopted Dainty as foster-mother, almost from the moment they were left together in the same enclosure. They feed together during the day and can be seen lying together at nights, the fox-red of Dainty's summer coat contrasting with the black-and-white coat of the kid, as they chew the cud together.

Remarkable enough as this may seem, a wild goat kid, hirsute in black-and-white and with, as yet, small but sharply pointed horns, lying with its adopted 'mother', a roe doe immaculate in summer red, the really incredible feature of Dainty's story is that Dainty chose voluntarily, and I must confess quite unexpectedly, to return 'home', while still at Culachy, after a long absence in the wild, and that she retained tameness and complete confidence in me in that interim period. Frankly, had anyone told me of such an occurrence I would have found it hard to believe. It *did* happen, however, to me and the living proof of it, Dainty herself, is lying, with 'her' kid, busily chewing the cud even as I write this.

6

The Forked Switch
A stag with an atrociously ugly head, and how he eluded the stalkers for three seasons

I FIRST saw the 'forked switch', as I came to call him, in late September 1955. We had been all day in Coire na Ceire, a wide, shallow coire, much broken up by peat hags. There we were engaged in an arduous, belly-crawling, painfully slow stalk on a stag, ensconced with his numerous hinds in an almost unassailable position. In the late afternoon, when we looked as if we were at last going to get near him, he upped and showed us his heels and those of his hinds, leaving us to wonder greatly.

Then we saw the skylined figures of two pony trekkers riding along the 'right of way' which bisects our ground, giving their scent to the whole coire. This at least explained matters, and if some rather harsh opinions were expressed about pony trekking in the stalking season perhaps we may be excused!

Our stag and his hinds went in a wide semicircle and ended up fairly high on the bare green slope to the south of the coire. It was getting late and we were far out, but one last attempt was tried. Getting into a convenient burn at the foot of the slope we worked our way up it, coming into view of the slope again higher up the burn, to see another stag, with a smaller herd of hinds, nearer to us than the one we had failed on. Putting the glass on him I saw that he was a most peculiar-looking switch, his antlers wide of span, with brow points and then nothing, until, on one top, there was a very small fork. A heavily bodied stag, and, with a head like that, better off the ground, and so we forthwith essayed to get him. The other deer were, however, still restive from their first alarm, and at last went away up the slope. The 'switch', all his wits about him, as I was later to know very well, took the hint at once, and in turn made off with his hinds. It was now too late to do anything, and we went home, tired, peat-blackened and stagless, and with a very jaundiced opinion of pony trekkers.

Three days later, on a day which was utterly ruined by legions of restless hinds, I saw the 'forked switch' again. He had no hinds that day and had either seen us or the hinds we had disturbed before we saw him. He was running along the face of the green slope where we had first seen him, stopping momentarily to roar, then resuming his gallop to vanish over the march at the ridge's summit. For various reasons the coire was left quiet for the rest of that season and I saw no more of the 'switch'.

By next season, that of 1956, I had almost forgotten him. On 17th September, after many fruitless days looking over bunches of hinds for shootable stags, we were coming along the summit ridge south of and above Coire na Ceire, just inside our march. Ahead, over a shallow rise on the ridge, we heard roaring, the first that season. What a change came over the day then, what fresh hopes, and what memories evoked of roaring last heard a full year ago. Creeping fast, but stealthily, to the top of the rise, we inched heads over until we could see, fifty yards on the wrong side of the march, my acquaintance of last year, the 'forked switch'. He was roaring lustily on the fringe of some thirty hinds, his head a facsimile of last year. We were even then within shot, the nearest I had yet been to the stag, but, wait as we did, in a perfect ferment of mounting anticipation, desire, and, eventually, frustration, the big fellow would not oblige us by coming in to our ground and, at last, driving his hinds before him, he was away!

The smug righteousness of temptation resisted was augmented later by a feeling of blissful relief when I learned from the stalker on the other ground that he and his 'rifle' had watched the whole tableau from a high, overlooking top, although too far away to try for the stag themselves. Their glasses had been glued on us, while, one imagines, they almost laid wagers as to whether we would transgress or not.

Four days later I approached the coire again, from the lower end this time, and 'glassed' its wide bowl of riven peat hags and runners. Lying almost in its middle was a small bevy of stags, and among them (by now beginning to be coveted) the head of my 'switch'. Well above them was a large herd of hinds, with no stag; below them, a sloping wide sweep of heather, its only cover the tangle of peat hags which carved it up. Retreating a bit into a burn which approached the bottom of the hags, we wormed our way into the start of them. Up them we crawled, here able to scurry, stooped double, up a deep runner; there, obliged to clasp black smelly bog to our bosom, until, breathless and peat-streaked, we inched to a torran's top, within shot of our stags, lying cudding peacefully ahead. A wait was indicated by our breathlessness, and to give a better chance when the stag (for only one was considered) got to his feet. The rifle, a beautiful weapon with a gleaming telescopic sight, was slid carefully over the torran's top, and we lay regarding our quarry. A stag rose at last (needless to say it was *not* the 'switch'), a second, then a third one, rose, grazing quietly, momentarily obscuring the 'switch' and thus causing a nervous dew to spring to our foreheads. The suspense was becoming a thing to be felt, stretching tautly between us; my 'rifle' wanted *a* stag, while I, wanting *only* the 'switch', prayed inwardly that *he* would rise before patience and endurance were exhausted. At last, glorious moment, he rose and presented a fair broadside, as he stood still on rising. The rifle was carefully aimed, and fired. The stag, alas, ran so fast that no second shot was possible; the first one had been a complete and inexplicable miss. Chastened, we carried on, to have another shot in the evening; and another miss—a day best forgotten.

The weather broke then, that year, and rain and mist, with spate-swollen burns, made that far-out coire out of the question; it was not until after the season's end that I saw my 'switch' again.

On 16th October I was going on a round of the forest, keen to see what stags were still in with us. A lot of roaring was coming from the head of Coire na Ceire, and even in the mist and grey light which prevailed that day I could make out a very large herd of hinds presided over by a big ten-pointer, a really good-looking stag. Crossing well below them I cut on to the green south face of the coire, along which my route lay. Ahead of me I heard a stag roaring, and in a moment picked him out, alone, dark against the green slope. Spying him, I saw it was the 'forked switch', roaring almost incessantly, now and again plucking a feverish mouthful; all the time, feeding or roaring, he was facing down into the coire across which could be dimly made out the far distant forms of the hinds

63

and their 'master' stag. It was not hard to read the story: he had been thrashed out and was loth to leave the vicinity of his erstwhile harem. I itched, rifleless though I was, to get nearer him; he stood fair athwart my route anyway, and there was nothing to be lost. The approach was impossibly devoid of cover, but the stag was absolutely engrossed in his rutting fever, and so, stopping when he stood silent at gaze, moving when he plucked grass or roared, I gradually got closer to him. At last, realizing now that with very great care I *could* get near him I really started stalking, belly-flat now, inching over the bare ground, till I reached the welcome concealment of a shallow, green fold, beyond which was the stag. Guided by his roars I advanced, crouched low, over the fold and crept up the gentle rise of it, to lie within thirty yards of the unsuspecting stag. This near, I could now see that he was in a pitiable state: his right eye, the one which had been towards me all the time, was almost shut, the gleaming, dark eye, opaque looking; from it a dark streak furrowed down his head where moisture had seeped, and indeed was still seeping. This, then, was why I had managed my 'masterly' stalk! With pride somewhat deflated I watched, and took a photograph of the battle-scarred stag. As he moved a pace forward he crippled badly on one foreleg. What a Homeric battle there must have been waged, with only the hinds as spectators, a scant few hours ago.

I had a new roll of film in my camera; thirty yards was, however, still too far away without a telephoto lens, and the light was shockingly bad. Emboldened by the stag's obvious blindness, as long as he continued to keep his right eye to me, I essayed to get to the cover of a small bump only ten yards from the stag. He neither heard nor saw me, deafened by his own persistent roaring and blind in his right eye, and I reached my scant concealment undetected.

As he lifted his head to gaze down the coire, the full ugliness of its shape could be seen, but as he turned it full on to me, to scratch with a hind leg at the itch of his wounded eye, its width could be admired, a width which many a stag with good points too often lacks. Lying with bated breath, watching (and surreptitiously photographing), the roaring of another stag, approaching from the coire, caused me to look that way. Up towards us, drawn by the roaring of the 'switch', came another stag, very slightly smaller of body, and with a narrow, nasty type of head. He, too, was crippling on one foreleg, another thrash-out! His pace slowed as he came near, and he stopped to roar. The 'switch' advanced a little way to meet him, and, turning inwards while still a little way from him, they both paced, stiff-legged as two belligerent terriers, up towards me, the 'switch' keeping always on the inside. I was apparently within his area of 'mastership'. Empty of hinds as it now was, he still apparently felt master of it. Reaching a level a bit above me, they turned as one and paced back, the 'switch' retaining his inside position. At the lowermost point of his apparent beat the 'switch' stopped. The other stag stopped in turn and faced round to the 'switch', hesitated for a moment or so, then making up his mind, turned again and crippled slowly off. Nothing to be gained here, from fighting a stag without hinds, or was the mettle of the half-blinded but still dauntless 'switch' too much for him? The 'switch' roared loud and long as his 'rival' departed, as if in triumph at his easy victory.

Shortly after this, my film finished and my body cramped and cold, I crawled back a little and rose to my feet. The 'switch' saw me with a start of surprise, and after a second's indecision made off, with his crippling gait, downhill. I carried on then, wondering whether his blindness was to be permanent or temporary, and if permanent, would he survive the winter? His foreleg would, no doubt, soon get better, but his eye? I doubted it. Had I my rifle I might have shot him then; as it was, I could only feel sorry for him in his present condition. He was a stag who wintered far down on the other side of our ground, only coming into our ground to rut, in the same part of the coire every year, as was now apparent; of his fate in the winter I would have no control or knowledge. I was left speculating and hoping.

The following year, 1957, I went around the forest towards the end of August. Being a hind forest, we usually had no big stags in early; plenty of hinds, and with them, stripling stags which had not yet joined the stag herds, but big stags, no! Coming along midway on the green face, where I'd photographed the blinded 'forked switch' last year, I spotted a large herd of hinds running in from the top, slanting diagonally across my front into the coire. At the rear were two or three small stags, and behind them an obviously large stag. What was a big stag doing in with hinds at this early stage? With the 'switch' very much in my mind now I swung my glass on to the stags. It was indeed the now familiar head, no different this year, and I was sure now, though I could not get nearer to verify it, that his being in with hinds and youngsters at this time could only mean that he had indeed been *permanently* blinded in that right eye last season. At this time he should have been with his fellow stags, higher out on the tops; instead, suffering from the disability of one sightless eye, he was in with the hinds and with stags very much junior to him.

The stalking had not started; when it did I took the first chance to come out to the coire. On 9th September, then, I came down from the top of the south green ridge, into the coire. We were a rather unwieldy stalking party that day (one which seldom pays dividends), four of us in all—stalker, the 'rifle' (a young lad), and his father and a friend as spectators. Coming down slowly towards the coire, a hiss from the father of the 'rifle' brought us to a sudden halt. Far below, in a cluster of hags on the slope, he had seen the antlers of a lone stag, lying down, his back, luckily, to us. There was no retreat up the bare green slope, and the 'rifle' and I started slithering down, belly-flat and head foremost in uncomfortable progress while our companions lay watching and debated our chances. Coming near the stag I 'glassed' his head which was all we could see of him. He was, as I'd suspected, the 'forked switch', now lying alone, morose in his disability. Slithering lower we lost sight of him, and had to climb a huge boulder to pinpoint him. Creeping quietly and cautiously down the winding hags which we had now reached, we got at last very close to him. Too close, perhaps, but lying low as he was, the configuration of the ground had him out of sight had we stopped farther out. The rifle was pushed carefully over the edge of our peat runner; the stag, some thirty yards away, hearing some slight noise, got up and stood motionless, looking round, a perfect 'broadside'. Grasping the knife in my pocket, in my own mind already gralloching the stag, I silently motioned the lad to take the shot. The 'switch' at once gave a bound out of sight below us, low in our tangle of hags as we were. Seizing the rifle and running to the edge of the ridge I saw him stopped, already far below, looking back. Almost at once he resumed his flight, going well, though I was sure he had been hit. He now had us in view at once if we moved at all after him, and as if aware of this, he swung in a wide arc below us, out over the open coire. Eventually, he disappeared among some birch trees fringing the main burn at the bottom of the coire. We pursued then, freed from our immobility, but a very long way behind, to catch one more fleeting glimpse of him far down the burn, and then to lose him, search as we would, in the thickening trees lower down the burn's course.

Next day the lad's father, who vowed that he had hardly slept, thinking of the stag, came out to try and get him. It turned into a day of torrential rain, an incessant, drenching, soul-destroying, glass-ruining downpour, but we carried on and searched the coire as well as the weather permitted. There were hinds and some small stags, but no sign was seen of the 'forked switch'. We went home soaked to the skin but satisfied we had done all that we could do.

A fortnight went by with no sign of the 'switch'. At last, on the 23rd of the month, I saw him again high on the face, as we stalked another lower stag, late in the evening. We got the stag we were after but the 'switch' had seen us long before and had 'lit out' as fast as ever I had seen a stag go; he was undoubtedly now sharpened to a keen edge by his recent narrow escape.

Next day it was the same tale. We came cautiously down the coire's burn to see a rapidly retreating 'switch' vanishing over the skyline, while his hinds, incredible as this may seem, had not seen a hair of us, and, undisturbed by the stag's rapid withdrawal, continued placidly grazing.

There followed a day's rest and on the 26th I tried the coire again; by now the 'switch' was almost an obsession and rapidly becoming legendary to the 'rifles' who stalked here. On this particular day I had a lady 'rifle', very keen and very quick of eye but a little handicapped by having to shoot off her left shoulder. We had an abortive stalk early on, then 'glassing' the area where the 'switch' rutted, I picked him up in his usual very ticklish position, with some thirty hinds. We started to stalk him, first up under cover of a burn, then a very difficult bit, up across a very open rushy slope into, we hoped, the cover of some hags below the deer. The wind denied us an approach from above, as it usually did in this coire. As we inched upwards, after leaving the burn, the deer almost inevitably saw some movement and, not very alarmed, drifted a little higher into a perhaps slightly better position. Slithering back into the burn we had a much overdue lunch, to give the deer time to settle, and again tackled them. It was now wearing on in the afternoon and as we wormed slowly up, the deer began slowly, then all at once quickly, to work down aslant us towards the coire. They would only just be in shot, and a quick one at that, before they got to windward of us, on their new course. Sliding round quickly the 'rifle' tried to get into position but just a fraction too late; the stag offered a split second chance just as the leading hind got our wind, then he was 'rump on' fleeing back up the hill; yet another win for the 'switch'!

More determined than ever, next day saw me with another 'rifle', a very consistently good shot, hurrying up the burn in the coire to cut off the 'switch' who was going to cross it above from his night feeding ground to his daytime position on the south face. Scarlet of face and scant of breath we reached a commanding torran, ahead of the deer. The 'switch', surely ours now, was walking slowly about a hundred yards off, stopping now and again to crop heather as he crossed our front. His breathing eased a bit, the 'rifle' took the shot at the broadside stag, to make the first miss he'd ever made with me. The astounded stag uncharacteristically stood for a second shot, to be missed again. In surprise and mortification the 'rifle' fruitlessly emptied his magazine at the now running stag, before I, silver bullets and charmed lives running through my mind, could restrain him. Later that day this same 'rifle' made a lovely shot, at longish range and with no time to spare, and dropped his stag, dead, with a bullet in the neck!

Going home in the evening I had a spy at the far-off north ridge of the coire. Surely that was the 'forked switch'? But what was he doing on ground a good mile distant from the usual stance? Perhaps the continual pursuit had caused him to shift. Saying nothing I decided to try again next day.

Accordingly, on the familiar route, out we came next day, a different 'rifle' again, a very hardy lady, a grand 'crawler' and a good shot; sooner or later the luck of the 'switch' must run out. Arriving at a place with a commanding view of the face where I had seen the 'switch' last evening, I glassed it thoroughly; there were the hinds but with a growing sense of despondency I could see no stag. Shifting a little higher up the slope I tried again. There he was, scarcely visible at that distance, lying down with only his antlers visible in a hag near his hinds. Sliding back we got down the nearby burn, then up another one to the base of a deep gully which ran almost to within shot of the deer. We walked up it, completely out of sight. The last bit was a very exposed crawl to within long shot of our quarry. Reaching this point safely we lay in position to await the rising of the couched stag. From where we now lay the deer were just below the top of the ridge, which flattened out over the top into an area of folds and peat hags. The deer lay quiet and unsuspicious. All at once the stag rose, and keeping his rump to us all the time, rapidly 'forked' hind after hind to her feet with his antlers and almost in the one motion drove them over the skyline out of sight. Words can hardly describe my feelings—the very Devil was in this stag!

No time was wasted in repining: we ran, crouching, to the ridge—no sign of the deer. We had to go on cautiously now; in the broken ground ahead we could easily 'jump' a lagging hind if we followed too recklessly. Fold after fold, peat hag after peat hag, we cautiously slipped through; inexorably the edge of the wide, broken plateau approached, and still no sight of deer. At its farther edge the ground dropped suddenly and steeply in a precipitous green face; stretching widely below was an expanse of heather and bog, in which no deer were to be seen. There remained one chance: the deer might still be, concealed by the slope's steepness, directly below us, at the base of the face. Craning cautiously outwards at the edge, we looked straight down; the deer were feeding quietly about eighty yards below, the stag among them, huge looking. It was a most difficult shot, head, shoulders and rifle out over space, pointing almost vertically down, at a vertigo-inducing angle, but it was taken dauntlessly and quickly, myself hanging on to the ankles of the 'rifle'. Scarcely able to believe it, I watched the stag drop to the shot and lie still. Jubilant, we hurried down to stand beside him in mutual congratulation while the hinds rapidly disappeared. Looking at him I was conscious of some disappointment; he was certainly big (eighteen stone as it turned out) but why did his head look so narrow? I had been so sure it was a really wide one. Turning his head I looked at his right eye; there was nothing wrong with it. So much for my hopes! He was undoubtedly a switch and there was the familiar small fork on one antler. Surely there could not be two so alike in the same coire? Stifling my unvoiced doubts I gralloched the stag while the 'rifle' went to signal the pony-man. On the way home my doubts grew. Why *had* he been rutting so far from his usual place, and on *what* antler had the small fork of 'my' switch been? Shocking admission as it is, I could not for the life of me remember clearly. The fork of this dead switch was on the right antler, I was practically sure the fork of 'mine' was on his left antler and I *was* sure of the blindness of the right eye. Reaching home I looked at last year's photographs and notes. All doubts were resolved; it was not *the* 'forked switch'. I was not done with him yet. I have no doubt whatever that the two stags were related, probably from the one sire. Their heads were identical in the number of points, but the small fork was on a different antler, and there was a big difference in width. At any rate, the dead stag was well rid of, and the season was not yet finished.

I was twice more in the coire before the season's end, but saw no sign of the 'forked switch'. The weather again turned foul towards the season's end and we had to content ourselves with lower ground. The coire needed a rest, anyway, as did my legs.

On 16th October I was on my usual annual post-stalking round. Spying the 'forked switch's' rutting area I saw a small herd of hinds lying among its hags. With quickening interest I 'glassed' the herd closely—there was my *bête noire*. Getting closer, up the burn below, I spied him carefully. I still could not get close enough to be sure of his right eye, but what I saw of his general condition made me at once decide to try for him myself, next day. He now looked shrunken and donkey-like, his coat a tufty red; in any case, it was high time his chances of handing down his atrocious head were ended.

Next day I set off early. By 9.30 a.m. I was in the coire, the time when normally we would just be leaving the lodge, two hours away. The deer were there, grazing very slowly upwards, the 'switch', roaring at intervals, with them. I had to take a great deal of care in coming up the burn bisecting the coire as herds of deer were on both sides; if even one lot went away so also would the vigilant 'switch'. At last I was up to where the really ticklish bit began, the long, flat wiggle up the shallow green incline, striving to bury myself in the longish grass and all too ocasional clumps of rushes. All the while I was in full view of the deer, until I reached the slightly better cover of the peat hags, a good hundred yards of which had to be wormed up, to where I would shoot from. With infinite care, an inch in an hour, lying still whenever a hind lifted her head from her grazing, I crossed the grassy incline and reached the dubious shelter of the hags. I could afford little time; the deer were still grazing slowly up and I had to resume my tortuous slither, this time up the peat runners. Heart beating, I freely admit, a good deal faster than usual, I was at last at the peat bank from where I was hoping to shoot. About a hundred yards out the 'switch' was feeding, three-quarters on, going slightly away from me, a mouthful or two, a slow step, then another leisurely crop at the heather. I slipped off the safety catch and aimed carefully. Momentarily, panic overcame me—

would I miss, too? I took my cheek off the rifle's stock and lay with eyes closed for a moment, then again took careful aim and squeezed the trigger. A hit: the bullet's 'thump' reached my ears. The stag lurched, then mutely and almost appealingly held up a dangling foreleg. D—! Had I made a 'broken foreleg shot'? I took aim again quickly, but just as I was doing so the stag fell, rolled on to his back, kicked his legs violently, and then lay still. Blessed relief permeated my very being, as I slowly rose to my feet and walked to him.

Yes, his head *was* wide; what a pity that noble span had such puerile points, and yes, his right eye *was* blind, the eyeball dry and shrivelled. There, evident too, was a slight bullet graze, not yet crusted over, just breaking the skin of his back; he *had* been hit on the 9th, then. Poor devil, he had had a rough time; his coat was harsh and staring and he was woefully thin, not the rutting thinness but a 'wasting' thinness. I doubt very much if he would have survived the hardships of winter again, but yet, indomitably, he had managed to collect and hold hinds. My feelings were mingled as I looked at him: exultation that I'd got him, regret for a very worthy adversary; regret too, for his terribly poor condition. Obviously he had not been thriving since his antler wounds of last season. The coire would be much the poorer in interest now that he was gone—ugly head or not; I had come in pursuit of him so often—but better for his absence in perhaps breeding others of his like. When I skinned the head at home to take off the frontal bone I discovered a deep indentation in between his eyes, pitting the skull bone; the antlers which had blinded him had also very nearly pierced his skull. The stag he had tangled with must have been indeed a 'bonny' fighter!

His head measured (as a matter of interest) thirty-three and three-quarter inches wide in inspan; in length it was thirty and a half inches; and in beam only four inches.

7

The Golden Eagle

THE golden eagle is *the* bird of the Highlands, to most of us the very spirit of the wild and rocky hills it chooses to nest on. How it managed to survive while we lost sea eagle and osprey I just do not know, for, to anyone with a practised eye, its eyrie can usually be 'picked up' especially when the young are in the glaringly obvious white down stage, a stage which lasts for a full month. It is also, unfortunately, simplicity itself to shoot the female eagle, who sits 'very tight' indeed when near the end of her very long incubation period. I will never forget a day spent in giving a stalker (of the old die-hard school) a hand at going round fox dens, work which has a thrill of its own, especially when one is young and not given to sorting out the rights and wrongs for oneself. Coming along a hill-side dotted with cairns of scattered rock the stalker said: 'Quietly now, there is an eagle's nest just ahead and she will likely be sitting tight.' He then took the lead and rounding a small outcrop he stopped, raising his gun as he did so. 'There it is,' he said, and I just had time, powerless to intervene, to see the huge structure of the eyrie barely thirty yards distant with only the head of the sitting bird visible, turned towards us in utter surprise. The shot came and the eagle rose upright with a last convulsive heave of her feet to tumble off the nest; striking the steep slope below, now only an inanimate bundle of dark brown, she rolled and tumbled down until stopped by the rocks of a scree below. That was in 1957, more than a hundred years of persecution having been suffered by the species by then.

A roe fawn will weigh 4 to 4½ lb. at birth.

Dainty, still at the early age when she trusted to stillness to avoid detection.

XXVI

My wife Margaret feeding Dainty, a congenial task.

Dainty, completely unafraid, with Rusty, a terrier of the author's.

Dainty at six weeks old, dapples fading but height still only that of the cow parsley in the foreground.

XXVII

Dainty's Houdini vanishing act under the iron gate.

XXVIII

Mutual affection; Dainty and her first fawn.

XXIX

Dainty and her young twins. Twins are as common as singles with roe deer.

Dainty and her 'adopted' kid.

XXX

XXXI

The 'forked switch' roaring; as he turned his head to scratch at his eye the full span of his antlers could be admired.

The 'forked switch' and the narrow ten-pointer.

The 'forked switch'; note the line of moisture-darkened hair below his injured eye.

XXXII

One is always conscious of the complete paradox notable in the writings of John Colquhoun in his most interesting book *The Moor and the Loch*, in which he tells of 'sport' and wildlife in the latter part of the eighteenth century and the early part of the nineteenth. Before shooting one female eagle by coming in above her eyrie, he says that 'the noble bird was sitting in perfect security and peace', security and peace alike shattered by his shot. Again he writes: 'I once witnessed a touching instance of the attachment of an eagle to her young, which, like the child of some bloodthirsty chief, alone had the power to touch the single chord of tenderness and love in the heart of its cruel parent. I had wounded her mortally as she flew from her eyrie, quite unconscious of her having hatched an eaglet. Next day she returned to the foot of the rock, although not able to reach her nest—the feelings of a mother being stronger in her savage breast than either the sense of present pain or the dread of further danger.' Thus the man who shot her.

John Colquhoun was no mean naturalist, in those days when naturalists were scarce, and yet he slew both sea eagle and golden eagle. He also writes of an expedition from his home to Loch Ba, Black Mount (on Rannoch Moor), especially to try and shoot a sea eagle which at that time nested in a tree on an island. The nest was occupied but in this case the female eluded him, though he was rowed across to the island and installed in a 'hide' within range of the nest. Of this nest he writes: 'I have enjoyed the rare luxury of seeing both eyries' (sea eagle on its island tree eyrie and golden eagle on its crag) 'at the same moment and both queens in undisturbed possession of their thrones.' Of the osprey he writes: 'A pair had their eyrie for many years on the top of an old castle on a small island in Loch Lomond. I am sorry to say I was the means of their leaving that ruin, which they had occupied for generations.'

Charles St John, another observant naturalist, whose book *The Wild Sports and Natural History of the Highlands* was first published in 1846, wrote in very similar vein. He writes of 'the royal bird', and says, 'it would be a great pity that this noble bird should become extinct in our Highland districts.' And yet, further on in this same book, he writes of being installed in a hide by a shepherd, near the carcase of a sheep, to wait for a pair of eagles. He shot one: 'The monarch of the clouds alighted at once on the sheep, with his broad breast not fifteen yards from me', and of the second he continues, 'She went wheeling round and round above the dead bird, turning her head downwards to make out what had happened. At times she stooped so low that I could see the sparkle of her eye and hear her low complaining cry ... I fired and dropped her actually on the body of the other. I now rushed out. The last bird immediately rose to her feet and stood gazing at me with a reproachful half-threatening look. She would have done battle but death was busy with her and as I was loading in haste she reeled and fell perfectly dead.' What a poignant passage in these last two sentences, and yet a man capable of such feeling carried on killing eagles and was probably one of the chief killers and nest robbers of the osprey, to the point of its extinction in the Highlands. Let it not be thought that nest robbing of rare species was practised only in the last century, in days when the thought of extinction of a species was undreamt of. Only think back to the robbing of the first osprey to attempt to breed in the Highlands again so that in later years the conspicuous nest had to be guarded day and night by the R.S.P.B. Even this guard did not save the nest from being robbed again in 1971, a sad reflection on our more 'enlightened' attitude to our wildlife in the twentieth century. There was also the case only a few years ago of the two egg-collectors who were apprehended in the Highlands after they had robbed two eagle eyries, taking a clutch of three eggs from one, a very rare size of clutch for a bird who usually lays two eggs and, fairly often in my experience over the last fifteen years, may lay only one. These men, apprehended mainly through the vigilance of George Waterston, the R.S.P.B. chief representative in Scotland, were later heavily fined, yet one of them had the cool audacity to ask for the two clutches of eggs back. Needless to say he did not get them.

In 1958 I really began to study eagles and keep records of what I will call Pair 'A' and Pair 'B'. In 1959 I started records of Pair 'D' and in 1962 of Pair 'C', so that I now have continuous records of the breeding success, or otherwise, for fourteen years in two cases, for thirteen in another and for ten years in the fourth. Readers will realize, in view of the egg-collecting paragraph, that I cannot be more specific than to say that all these pairs nested in the Monadhliaths on adjacent territories, territories which covered an immense tract of 'wild Highlands'.

Eagles are early nesters, laying an egg, or eggs, in late March, eggs which usually hatch in early May, the young then being on the eyrie until July. The earliest I have seen a young eaglet leave the eyrie has been 8th July, the latest 24th July.

Of the occupied eyrie of Pair 'A' I wrote in 1958: 'The eyrie was situated in a roughly triangular cleft splitting a relatively small rock face, resting on a jumble of "rotten" unstable rock slabs which, I imagine, had at one time come away from the face to create the cleft above. Its five feet or so of structure raised it well up into the cleft, its actual nest cup being in the shelter of an over-hang which made observance from above only possible by craning well out over the drop, toes well "dug in" to the soft turf of the ledge above. From the north side of the eyrie one could get to within eight feet of the nest edge, balancing in a rather precarious attitude, one hand clinging hard to a crack in the rock and one foot on a small tufty ledge. (This was my "camera" position at this eyrie so that, balancing as I was, I had to operate the camera with one hand, a procedure not calculated to ensure good photographs.) From below one could get to the base of the eyrie easily enough but owing to the unstable nature of the rock I did not trust it enough to climb sufficiently high to look into the nest. The nature of the rock cleft sheltered the eyrie completely on its east and south sides while on the north a rock buttress sheltered and concealed it except from my "human fly" camera viewpoint. The west exposure was the only "open" side and it overlooked the glen and its river far below. Above, below and to each side of the eyrie outcrop stretched a very steep green slope broken up by similar outcrops or by aprons of treacherous, sliding grey scree, at times of small rocks, at others of rocks of some considerable size. For quite a distance below the eyrie the steep slope was littered by sticks and vegetation which had been dropped, over the years, while refurbishing the huge eyrie: crowberry, blaeberry, tufts of heather and great woodrush among it. Directly below the eyrie were tufts of greenery with downy feathers caught in them which had probably been knocked or blown off the eyrie in the lengthy incubation period.'

This eyrie was the one on which the female had been shot in the previous year, and yet the male had brought his new mate to it. There is a belief, largely true, that an eagle will not use the same eyrie site in two successive years, and so this probably accounted for the eyrie 'escaping' in 1958. To this belief I myself subscribed until these last three years in which, for the first time, I personally wit-nessed, in the case of *two* pairs of eagles, eyries used in two successive years. One pair, Pair 'B', has three eyrie sites, and the other pair, Pair 'C', has five sites to choose from. In the preceding eleven years I had never seen an eyrie, from which the young had flown success-fully, used in two successive years, and I would have definitely told any inquirers that it never occurred except in the case of a pair with *only* one site (a rare occurrence), or in the case of an eyrie where the eggs had not hatched *or* the young had perished at a very early stage, due to the death of the female or some other cause (e.g. addled eggs). This was one more instance to me of how unwise it is to be dogmatic about our wildlife, no matter how much knowledge we may think we have.

Of this 1958 eyrie I wrote on 15th June: 'I came in from above, and as I lay above the eyrie for a momentary rest I heard a tearing, crackling noise from the eyrie. The female must be on, unseen below me, tearing up prey to feed the single eaglet. Craning outwards, almost quivering with excitement, I looked straight into the eyes of the female eagle, fierce and unwinking, boring into me. Her head and neck feathers were of pale yellow-gold, and her tremendous beak had a tiny piece of shredded grouse flesh clinging to its hooked tip—flesh from the partly eaten grouse which she was standing on, both enormous feet (yellow, with black talons, and feathered all the way down the leg to the spread of the foot) holding it down for its dissection. There were lighter, pale brown patches on her back and wings, probably "older" feathers not yet replaced in the moult. For a long moment her eyes bored into me before she turned, and in one and the same motion flung herself off the eyrie.'

By 8th July the eaglet was virtually fully fledged though fugitive wisps of down clung here and there among its back feathers. It was now strong on its legs and active, spreading its huge wings and lung-ing at my walking stick as I prodded at the remains of a grouse near to it. Not far below the eyrie a red deer hind, her 'new' dappled calf and her calf of the previous year (in Highland terms her 'follower') grazed, quite unalarmed by the proximity of the occupied eyrie and quite unaware of my presence. So near were they that I could hear the hind's teeth audibly grinding away at some moss she had 'skinned' from off a rock. She was handsome in her new, red summer coat and her calf even more attractive in its juvenile dappled coat, but the 'follower' was still in her old winter coat, bleached almost white and with ragged loose tufts of hair spread untidily through it, at which she nuzzled at intervals, causing loose hairs to float lazily away on the light breeze while some remained clinging to her moist dark muzzle. On my way out that day I had watched two young dappled calves come slanting up the slope near where I sat unsuspected. One was very noticeably yellow-brown below its dapples while the other seemed thicker set and with the more normal red-brown background to its spots. The yellow-brown one was leading and was obviously 'the boss', for at one stage of their journey up by me she (for I believe it was a female) turned on the other, and smacking it with one hard-hoofed foreleg, made it take the lead until she decided to take over the leadership again. There was no hind near to them at all, though I had put a small lot of eight hinds and three calves on ahead of me only minutes before. The two calves were probably about a month old and should certainly have been able to outrun a fox but just as certainly they would have been easy prey for the eagle. However, in all the years I watched occupied eyries of Pair 'A', deer calf *never* featured, though it did on the eyries of the two neighbouring pairs, Pairs 'B' and 'C'.

On the rowan tree which grew out of the cliff on the north-west side of the eyrie and its huge occupant, a tiny willow warbler flitted that day from branch to branch in its search for insects, obviously in no awe of its predatory neighbour—'the "lion" and the "lamb" together'.

I went out again on 15th July, a dull drizzly day, in the still, moist air of which the lovely aromatic scent of the carpet of wild thyme I was treading on, on the last stretch to the eyrie, rose refreshingly to my nostrils. At the eyrie, the eaglet was still there, rather to my surprise, and was surrounded by ample 'feeding stuffs'. A headless rabbit and three young grouse lay on the now tawdry, trampled surface of the nest. The eaglet was very active, and for the first time he used his huge talons, instead of pecking with his beak, when I poked with my stick at one of the grouse. When I pulled my stick free from his foot, using some considerable force, he grabbed it instantly with the other, using a 'hand over hand' action. His legs were now well-feathered, right down to the feet, a yellow-white in colour, plentifully streaked with light brown, his head a coppery, red-brown which would turn golden as he grew older. The rest of his plumage was a rather dull, dark brown with no sign of the handsome breast markings of the common buzzard.

Walking out in the early morning that day I startled a roe buck into hurried flight, even in his hurry managing to look graceful in his lithe bounds, disappearing and reappearing, a lovely fox-red, amid the deep 'sea' of green bracken which covered the slope below my path.

The eaglet was still there on 23rd July but on 28th July I reached the eyrie to find it empty, recently so, as a fresh green sprig of heather and one of blaeberry lay beside the hindlegs of a rabbit. The eyrie was desolate looking, its brown, trampled surface sloped away on its north-west edge, obviously the favourite edge of the eaglet, as if in imminent danger of falling away. No wonder fresh structure is needed whenever an eyrie is used again. A variety of small breast feathers of plucked prey, with one or two larger breast feathers of one or other parent, clung to the eyrie structure tangled in its sticks, while the slope below was streaked and splashed with the 'whitewash' of the eaglet's evacuations.

As I went down home along the glen, conscious of a feeling of loss mingled with relief that my long early morning tramps were over for this nesting season, I saw an adult eagle high above, a farewell look for that year.

The prey seen at that eyrie consisted of grouse, rabbit, ptarmigan, ring-ousel, blue hare and black water vole.

Greenery used in adornment or freshening of the eyrie consisted of rowan, birch, dwarf willow, sphagnum moss, blaeberry, crowberry and heather.

In that year, 1958, I was not yet studying Pairs 'C' or 'D'. As for Pair 'B', the female was believed to have been shot. On a complaint being made, police investigated and found empty twelve-bore shotgun cartridge cases below the eyrie.

In 1959, Pair 'D' reared one eaglet and Pair 'A' also reared one, on an eyrie new to me, but to which I made regular visits until the eaglet flew. Pair 'B', the most vulnerable of the four pairs, in its proximity to habitation, again had the female shot.

The eyrie which Pair 'A' used was some two miles farther out than the one used in 1958 and it was much higher on the hill face, the final approach being up an almost vertical heathery rock-strewn face. This eyrie was unknown to the stalker on that estate but it *had* been known to the older stalkers, for my old friend and predecessor at Culachy, Johnny Kytra (see *Highland Deer Forest*) knew of it. The eyrie was built on a small great-wood rush-grown ledge; about three feet of new structure had been built up on about a foot of very old compacted heather. The new structure was mainly of heather with some dead sticks among it and the 'decor' on it was of dwarf willow, rowan, crowberry and cowberry. Definitely the best concealed eyrie of this particular pair, it was invisible from the glen below, and from above because of its overhang; from the north side a rock outcrop concealed and sheltered it; to its south side a large rowan tree, growing from the rocky face of a gully, completely hid it. I was able to get right to the edge of this eyrie.

The single eaglet it held was about a month old and obviously thriving, still clad entirely in white down. Some bloodstained bones and feathers of both grouse and ptarmigan gave indication of the prey.

As a matter of interest I found this eyrie by sweeping the face on which it was situated with my stalking 'glass', from high on the opposite face.

Five days later I again made the long trudge out to the eyrie, leaving home at 4 a.m. As I approached the eyrie at around 6.30 a.m., and while I was yet about half a mile from it, the female (I assumed) flew from the vicinity of the eyrie and glided across the glen without once flapping her wings, to swing round, still gliding, and go along the opposite face of the narrow glen. I heard the eaglet 'cheeping', that ridiculous farmyard chicken noise which this huge bird uses, as I scrambled up the last arduous steep to the eyrie's edge. It showed the first dark, almost black-looking tips of feathering now, mostly on wing and tail edge. The female had evidently been on the nest to feed it, for its crop bulged out like a soiled tennis ball and the remains of a grouse lay beside it.

The eaglet's eye was already quick; it cocked its head to one side and looked upwards, and following its gaze, I saw an adult eagle gliding high above. As I watched, two common gulls appeared and began to pester it, giving tongue in gull language while the eagle glided serenely on.

The slopes below the eyrie, as I now had leisure to see on my way down, were patterned in yellows, blues and reds, of bird's foot trefoil, milkwort and wild thyme. Here and there the less flaunting but still attractive flowers of alpine lady's mantle and mountain everlasting showed to the discerning eye, and directly below the eyrie, obvious to the eye of discerning and undiscerning alike, the flamboyant spikes of rose bay willow herb thrust up, almost to the eyrie's base. I have never been able to work out the connection between rose bay willow herb and golden eagle eyries but connection there most definitely is, for in the remote heather, short grass and rock-strewn high hill faces, I have personally found it only directly below the eyries of all four pairs of 'my' study eagles. Does the eagle take in some form of prey, bird or mammal, of which the seeds of rose bay willow herb form part of its diet, and do these seeds pass through the eaglet to be evacuated onto the face below; or does this very evacuation, daily for ten to twelve weeks, create a 'burnt' condition under which the long dormant seeds of the willow herb germinate? One other plant 'mystery' is easier to solve, the sporadic appearance of nettles in isolated clumps throughout the hill, only by old ruins, fox dens, or badger setts, i.e., where the foot of man has 'carried' the seed.

My next visit was in mid-June, leaving home as usual at 4 a.m., a grey morning, with red-tinged sky to the east forecasting the rising of the tardy sun. The long journey was as usual enlivened by the sight of deer, a sight which the early riser is rewarded by seeing, while his more lethargic (or wiser) brethren are still asleep. Within a mile or so of the nest two red deer hinds moved up the steep green face on my right hand. The first had a tiny, dappled sprite valiantly toiling behind her while the second hind was 'heavy' in calf, so near her time in fact that she soon halted, unable to take the steep face with her usual facility. Turning my eyes back to the first I saw that she was now alone; her calf had also seemingly decided that such steep going was not for it. It had lain down and I could not detect its resting place. There it would remain, lying 'doggo' until its departing mother arrived back in the evening, when her low-pitched call would cause her calf to materialize out of the 'empty' hill, eager for its feed of milk, short tail wagging in ecstasy as it sucked, with now and again a hard dunt with its domed forehead, lifting the haunch of the mother off the ground in its efforts to make milk flow more freely.

At about six weeks old the eaglet was feathering fast, and beside it lay the fresh untouched carcase of a blue hare. Beside the hare a headless ptarmigan had had its crop packed to bursting point with unripe, green blaeberries, blaeberry leaves and a few crowberry leaf tips—no sign of the adults at all while I was at the eyrie.

On my way back I sat for a while in the glen bottom to eat an apple and have a breather. My presence was obviously viewed with some apprehension, for a family of immature wheatears incessantly 'chack-chacked' at me from their stronghold of a nearby scree,

80

and near the river edge an anxious sandpiper intoned its plaintive 'wee-eep' note, bobbing in marionette style meantime, from its post on a large rock. I remembered seeing only a few nights ago, when coming home in the grey dimness which passes for dark in the Highland June after a long day at a fox den, a young but fully fledged sandpiper half-fluttering, half-swimming over a shallow pool in the burn ahead of me.

On 20th June of that year I again left home at 4 a.m. to visit the eyrie, this time to have an all-day session at it, or rather to observe it from a hiding place on the opposite side of the glen with my stalking glass. I arrived at the eyrie at about 6.15 a.m. with a fitful sun now shining, now obscured by grey cloud. The eyrie was brown and withered looking and already beginning to slope away on its outer edge. The eaglet was sheltering in the inner corner of the eyrie from the strong westerly wind which, even as I arrived, blew a large tuft of withered heather from off the eyrie's outer edge. It drew itself erect as I reached the eyrie's edge, opening its wings and clapping them shut in threat display. There was no prey, except a bloodstained breast bone of grouse or ptarmigan, visible on the nest.

I left the eyrie at 7.15 a.m. and instead of going home I crossed the river in the glen bottom and toiled up through the rough, broken scree and huge rocks which littered, chaotically so, the glen face opposite the eyrie. Reaching, by 8 a.m., a point almost opposite the eyrie, where a jumble of huge rocks gave me convenient cover from the eyes of the parent eagles, I thankfully shed my bag with its two cameras and a telephoto lens. I found that from this concealed viewpoint I had a very good view with my stalking glass of eaglet and eyrie. The eaglet, my disturbing presence gone, was now preening its feathers, back, wing and lower breast. At intervals it would halt its preening and scan the sky above, as if looking for a parent bird. At 8.20 its expectations were realized when one of the parents flew in, touched down, and took off again instantly. I distinctly heard the eaglet 'cheeping' in eager anticipation of 'breakfast at last', but whatever prey had been carried in, it was too small for me to identify, distant as I was from the eyrie. The eaglet looked after the departing adult as if wondering why it had gone so quickly, then, as if metaphorically shrugging its shoulders, turned its attention to a more important matter, food. I could see the characteristic stooping and rising erect movement of the feeding bird of prey, as it held the prey (still indistinguishable to me) down with its feet and tore it into eatable fragments with its 'knife and fork', the powerful hook-tipped beak. At one moment, as it turned broadside to me, I could see in the strong sunlight now full on the eyrie its beak opening and shutting as it ate, a feather clinging to it. Twice I saw it tear off and swallow what were obviously large pieces, coming erect to do this, and gulping repeatedly before it got the food down. By 8.50, it seemed to have satisfied its appetite and it began to preen its feathers again. Ten minutes later, however, it resumed its 'attack' on what was left of the prey, getting a bit of fluff stuck to its beak as it did so, shaking its head, as if in annoyance, until it got rid of it. A further five minutes later it ceased feeding, and backing to the nest edge, it projected powerfully into space a liquid white jet. Bodily needs for the time being satisfied, the eaglet, drowsy after its meal, retired to the innermost corner of the eyrie and went to sleep.

Some blackface sheep, ewes and lambs, were all this time grazing unconcernedly around the eyrie site, some not more than 300 yards from it.

At 10.30 a.m. as I was brewing some tea, an adult eagle glided, from north to south, along the length of the ridge above the eyrie, head bent down as if scanning the ground below for prey. Half an hour later, at about 11 a.m., the eaglet awoke, obviously feeling uncomfortable in the heat of the full rays of the sun, which had been beating on the eyrie since 8 a.m. Now restless, the eaglet went from one edge of the eyrie to the other, beak gaping open, looking up, skywards, repeatedly. At one moment it stood on the eyrie's edge and extended its wings, half-open, as if to let air in between wings and body.

Shortly after this I left my viewpoint to thread my way down across the river and toil slowly up the steep face to the eyrie again, at which I arrived at about 1 p.m. The eaglet greeted me with open beak and an angry clap of its wings, then, very obviously more distressed by the lack of shade on the sunlit eyrie than by my presence, it stood, wings half extended and beak gaping, a large bead of moisture rolling periodically out of a 'nostril' orifice, down over the powerful beak to drip from the hooked tip. There was nothing left of the prey except a dusky feather or two from which it was impossible to identify it. Before I left the eyrie an adult came gliding over, to turn and glide low above me, head bent down scrutinizing what should have been a familiar figure by now. Despite the heat there was no offensive smell of prey remnants from the eyrie, though a few bluebottles were buzzing around it.

It was on a later visit to this eyrie that I first heard the 'yelping' of an eagle, a sound which I now believe to be one of irritation and annoyance. Hearing it first, and not being able to locate the source of it, my slightly guilty conscience led me to think it was my anti-eagle colleague out with his terriers on a fox den round, the sound was so like that of a terrier yelping in excitement. I had every reason to believe the querulous yelping of the adult eagle to be of displeasure, for the next time I heard it was as I was poised precariously at the eyrie and the female patrolled past, using her wings (i.e. not gliding), so close to the face to which the eyrie clung was she, alternately above and below the eyrie, giving me my best close-up view of an adult eagle since I began seriously to watch eagles. A little later that day she gave me even more reason to remember it, for she swooped at me three times as I was engrossed in photographing her eaglet, surprising me so much that I almost lost balance in the involuntary jump I made. This aggressive behaviour towards humans is definitely not typical of the species as a whole, however, for this has only happened to me in two seasons, out of fourteen spent watching eagles, and by two different females. Strangely enough this aggressive behaviour never came when the young were small and helpless but when they were almost fledged, and indeed in one case (as described fully in *Highland Deer Forest*) after the eaglet had left the eyrie.

The eaglet was still on this eyrie on 15th July, though it looked fully fledged and capable of flying. I had left home slightly later that day and now, mid-July as it was, the early morning chorus of the smaller birds was hushed and the stillness of early morning was only broken by the shrill 'mewing' of a circling buzzard, and the deep, guttural 'cronk-cronk' of a raven as it winged its way down the glen.

A meadow pipit rose in alarm, positively shrieking, almost from underfoot, as I neared the eyrie, and at my next step forward a young meadow pipit shot out of the grass ahead of me. It was evidently not yet at flying stage but so steep was the slope that it found itself involuntarily airborne, and it descended a good fifty yards, half-fluttering, half-parachuting, cheeping its dismay, legs dangling and beak, still with the light-coloured raised edges of immaturity, wide open. As it 'crash-landed' it was immediately encircled, as if in succour, by three adult pipits, while the original adult continued her agitated fluttering, in very real alarm, near me, where the rest of her young must have been.

The screes below the eyrie had some individual grey stones patched purple now with the droppings of the birds, probably mainly ring-ousels, which had been feasting on the ripe blaeberries, of which I had my share also as I climbed the steep by them.

A friend from Aberdeen, Gordon Smith, came to stay for a week-end with us and on 19th July I took him with me as he was very keen to see an eagle. I was exceedingly doubtful of our prospects of finding the eyrie still tenanted, and it was with a thrill of exultation for Gordon's sake that I saw the eaglet, back to us, engrossed in tearing at his early breakfast, the hinder half of a rabbit. It now looked magnificent, a lovely sheen on its feathers, all wisps of down gone. Gordon went right up to the edge of the eyrie and as he did so the eaglet positively sprang across the eyrie to stand menacingly between its half-rabbit and the edge where Gordon stood. I wanted a photo of Gordon at the eyrie and the only way to do this was to climb the large rowan immediately south of the nest. This I did and then asked Gordon to photograph me at the nest. I don't think I wrong Gordon in saying that he was unwilling to climb quite as high in the tree as I had done but at least he did tackle it. While he was climbing, the eaglet made one or two bowing motions, a curtsy to space, as it were. It crossed my mind that it might be about to fly but I over-confidently dismissed the idea. The sight and sound, the cracking and creaking of the rowan under the assault of Gordon's six feet four inches and size ten boots was, however, all too much for the eaglet, ready as it was to fly anyway. It again made its curtsy, thrusting head and neck out as it did so, and launched out into space, unfolding immense wings and flying with unexpected expertise, straight and true, right across the glen. I expected it would im-mediately pitch clumsily on the rock and heather of the opposite face but no, it turned skilfully to fly along the face, landing neatly on a large rock.

It was absolutely thrilling to watch this, the maiden flight of the eaglet I had watched for so long, and to see this early mastery of what must have been an unfamiliar element to it.

I felt a sense of loss as we turned from the brown, flattened mass of the eyrie with its half-rabbit, uneaten after all, but also a sense of elation in having seen the eagle exchange the vulnerability of the eyrie for the relative safety of the sky.

Prey at the 1959 eyrie of Pair 'A' consisted of grouse, ptarmigan, rabbit, blue hare and (suspected) ring-ousel.

Decor consisted of rowan, dwarf willow, heather, crowberry, cowberry, great wood rush and dry green moss (i.e. not sphagnum).

8

The Golden Eagle, continued

THE normal clutch of the golden eagle is two, but even if the two eggs hatch it does not by any means always follow that both eaglets will be successfully reared, for quite often one may die or perhaps be actually killed by its stronger nest mate. Should the latter happen it is usually within ten days to a fortnight after the eggs hatch. In other cases, when prey is scarce at the second crucial stage in the eaglet's life, of six to seven weeks old, the weaker of two eaglets (which has survived its six or so weeks of life simply because the female actually feeds both young more or less impartially), ceases to benefit from this impartiality because, from the six- to seven-week-old stage, until the young leave the nest, the prey is simply brought in by both adults and left for the young to feed themselves. When this happens, if one eaglet *is* stronger than the other, it will monopolize prey brought in, and if this prey is scarce, the weaker one grows progressively weaker as the stronger one grows stronger. The inevitable climax of this struggle for existence is the death by slow starvation of the weaker eaglet. However, perhaps because of the relative scarcity of prey in the north-west Highlands nowadays, some pairs of eagles lay only one egg, an instance being Pair 'A' in my study area where the clutch size has always been one egg only.

In 1960 Pair 'A' did not breed (I believe the female was killed); Pair 'B' laid two eggs; Pair 'C' I had not yet started studying; Pair 'D' laid one egg and reared one eaglet. Pair 'D', being farthest away from my home, I did not visit very often, concentrating on Pair 'B', which was a mere two hours from home.

I did not get out until 22nd May 1960 to investigate a site 'new' to me and unknown to the estate stalker. My notes read: 'Out early this morning (Sunday) to investigate a "suspected" eyrie site of Pair "B", neither of the two "known" sites being occupied (just as well as they had meant the death of two females in two successive years). An eagle came high above me as I was on the last stage of my walk to the suspected eyrie site, giving me fresh hope that the "new" eyrie might be occupied. Nearing it, I sat down and spied across at it at approximately 5 a.m. and saw, with a thrill of gratification, another eagle, the female by its size, poised on the edge of the eyrie. She flew off even as I watched and I sprang to my feet, fresh vigour inspired in me by the near certainty now that the "new" eyrie *was* occupied. The last steep pull to the eyrie was pretty arduous but I was amply rewarded. I was thrilled beyond measure to see two eaglets, still at the completely white, down-clad stage, by their size about three weeks old. It was not possible to get to the edge of this eyrie, built high up on a crag on a great wood rush-clad ledge, not a large eyrie in depth of structure—only about a foot high— but a fairly wide one, sheltered as usual by a slight overhang above and by buttresses of rock to east and west, only open on its north side. A trifle disappointed in this, after my "close ups" in the previous year, I found that I could choose a viewpoint directly above the nest or one at its west side from which, however, the inner corner of the eyrie was hidden. Above, I chose then, with its full view of the eyrie directly below, even though it meant craning far out over space to clear the overhang. I eventually rigged up a thin rope secured to a peg in the ground near the cliff edge, through which I could thrust one arm to the elbow, giving me at least moral support, while I operated my camera. On that eyrie that day there were the remains of four grouse, all roughly plucked. The eaglets were lying dozing, probably already fed, early as it was, by the female, before I'd arrived.'

A couple of weeks later I recorded at this eyrie prey (to me) most unusual, a large stoat, a rank and stringy mouthful or so, even for the not very choosy eaglets.

On 19th June a further prey 'surprise' awaited me, the remains, tail, hindquarters and a bloody, furless bit of forequarter, of a fox, an adult one at that. The backs of the somnolent eaglets were now almost completely clad in dark brown feathers with lighter brown beginning to streak the still predominant white of their heads.

June 26th was very misty; so thick was it that I had difficulty finding the eyrie crag. The mist which had hidden the crag from me had also hidden me from the female eagle. She did not see me until I was directly below the eyrie, when she flung herself off, swooping fairly low before she really got airborne, huge and black-looking in the mist. The eaglets lay together, the head of one cushioned, a macabre touch, on the nude carcase of a plucked grouse.

Yet another 'first' as far as prey was concerned came a week later. Lying below the eyrie crag but quite some way from it, was the foreleg of what had been a very young red deer calf. The pathetically tiny hoof was quite black, and some grains of peat were clinging to its under surface, showing that the calf had been at least a day old and not a still-born one. The two eaglets were lying replete on the eyrie platform, the smaller with its head resting on the other's tail. A part-eaten unplucked grouse lay near them; they were now at the age when they were expected to tear up food brought in by the parents to feed themselves.

As I sat above the eyrie crag that day an adult eagle appeared, her head glinting straw-yellow in the sunlight, gliding over a lochan a good mile from the eyrie. She started spiralling upwards as I watched, fascinated, climbing higher and yet higher in widening spirals. Watching, eye glued to my stalking glass, I saw the sun light up breast and black feathers alternately as she spiralled, glinting all the time on her head of pale gold. Out of nowhere, suddenly, arrived a small chestnut-red fury, a hen kestrel, narrow pointed wings fairly cleaving the air as she stooped at the great eagle. What dauntless courage, inspired by the 'madness' of maternity, to attack such a huge adversary, even although it *was* 'trespassing' over the kestrel's nest territory. Time after time she stooped at the eagle, and each time she did so the imperturbly gliding eagle flapped its huge wings upwards once and poked head and hooked beak upwards at the kestrel. Once she dropped her huge taloned feet, as if in uncontrollable irritation, but she did not cease her gliding nor counterattack her small adversary. The seemingly effortless speed at which her gliding was carrying her could be judged by the lightning flicker of the kestrel's wings necessary to keep her even within stooping distance of the eagle. After a few moments of this, while I watched and marvelled, the eagle had had enough and went into a long,

A trio of red deer stags.

Hind and calf in the Highlands, late summer.

XXXIII

Though two young golden eagles may often be hatched, both do not always
survive to reach flying age.

The female tenderly proffering a titbit to the hungry eaglet.

XXXV

Close up of a six-week-old eaglet.

XXXVI

A single eaglet of about seven weeks old.

The young eagle after its first flight from the eyrie.

XXXVIII

Power personified, a fully fledged young eagle.

XL

A substandard addled egg compared with a normal eagle egg.

Utter disgust and disappointment on Michael's face on seeing an unhatched egg and the shell of a second one.

shallow, fast glide, leaving the maternally inspired kestrel far behind, fast as she flickered her wings. Seconds only were sufficient to take the eagle from over the kestrel's 'territory', and the kestrel was apparently satisfied, as well she should have been, for she disappeared as quickly as she had materialized.

My visit on the following Sunday saw a complete reversal of the roles of hunter and hunted, sheer coincidence, but a rewarding one for me. As I sat above the eyrie after photographing the two eaglets, now fully feathered, with the prey, the picked-bare carcase of a blue hare and the two forelegs and one hindleg of a red deer calf, a kestrel came flying straight and fast by the crag. Behind it came the eagle, to my surprise, fairly driving herself through the air on powerfully wielded wings. She rapidly overhauled the kestrel, now screeching on a high note of panic, and small blame to her, for the eagle stooped at her, a tremendous 'swoosh-swoosh' of displaced air clearly audible to me. Whether only in warning or a miss I could not tell but at any rate it satisfied the eagle, who turned back then, leaving a deathly scared and no doubt relieved kestrel to disappear from the proximity of the eyrie.

At this eyrie the more 'forward' eaglet flew on 16th July and its nest mate not till a week later on the 23rd, a difference in courage and not capability, for both were indistinguishable in size after they were fully fledged.

Prey at this 1960 eyrie of Pair 'B' was varied to say the least: grouse, stoat, fox, blue hare and deer calf. Of decor I only saw a sprig or two of fresh rowan; this pair were not 'house proud'.

In 1961 Pair 'A' were re-established, the male having got another mate; one egg was laid and the resulting 'chick' successfully reared. Pair 'B' again successfully reared two young but the female of Pair 'D' was, I heard, shot. Pair 'C' I was still not visiting.

Pair 'A', being my 'home' pair and the one of which I had the longest continuous record, was the one I chose to make regular visits to, even although it was, in 1961, the farthest out of all the seven eyrie sites which the glen held.

I made my first visit on 2nd May after having done the round of all the other sites. Despite the fact that I had now been watching young eagles for four years it was still a thrill to find an occupied eyrie. On this eyrie, which had not been occupied for at least five years, there slept, in the still obvious nest cup, a tiny, white, down-clad eaglet, pink skin still showing below its 'thistledown' coat. As usual the eyrie was sheltered by an overhang, a low one in this case, under which the eaglet used to creep as it grew older. It was completely open to the south while the rocky arms of its crag sheltered it from east and west. Grouse was the prey on 2nd May, and grouse and rabbit formed the prey on the 9th. I visited the eyrie, into which I could easily look from above at a range of a few feet, again on 16th May. When within sight of the crag it was sited on I saw an adult eagle gliding high above it. By the time I was nearing the crag's top the eagle had vanished, but a black 'knob' did not seem to fit into my previous 'mind picture' of the skyline on which it showed. As I halted for a brief rest I heard the raucous 'screaming' of common gulls and then saw them, four in number, swooping and diving to the sound of their own outcry, over the black 'knob' on the skyline. A moment later an eagle appeared gliding along the ridge on which my black 'knob' was still apparent; perhaps it was not an eagle after all. My doubts were dispelled the next moment, when the black 'knob' took wing for a short flight, returning almost at once to its appearance of being simply a black 'knob', once more, on the skyline.

On the eyrie there lay a decapitated plucked grouse, a hen, as shown by a chain of small egg yolks and one complete egg, shelled but still white, devoid of all pigment. It had been heavily infested by tapeworm, a length of which was draped by it. The eaglet was now considerably larger than the grouse, whereas on my first visit it had been very considerably smaller than a grouse. The eyrie was now just a platform, all trace of 'cup' had disappeared.

Throughout my visits the eaglet continued to thrive unmolested. On a dull, dreich misty day in early June, I visited the eyrie to find a fresh fox cub, about four to five weeks old, lying dead on it. The cub had been 'plucked' almost bare and a foreleg and most of the head had been eaten. I managed to hook it out of the eyrie with my stick and did a post mortem on it. A vixen cub, her stomach was full of rodent fur, small bones, and undigested quill-ends of a small bird. The eaglet, most of its body plumage a dark sober brown now, while its head was a 'pepper and salt' mixture, was quite dry despite the continuous drizzle, due to the shelter of the low overhang.

I made the long trip out to the eyrie again, near the end of June. Families of longtailed tits were 'churring' noisily and flitting without pause in the tree-clad lower glen, seeming as numerous as the leaves they were so busily working among. I came in quietly above the eyrie without its occupant hearing me and surprised it doing wing exercises, extending them fully and flapping vigorously, all the time facing into space, its back to me. Another fox cub, practically all eaten, by its size from the same litter as the one of 6th June, lay on the eyrie.

Returning home that day I disturbed some hinds among some scattered birch trees. Two tiny calves strove to keep up with their mothers, dappled miniatures, richly coloured compared to the bleached, yellow-white, old winter hair still predominate on the mothers. Heads outstretched and fragile-looking, spidery legs pumping frantically, they kept up well, while still in my view at any rate.

Yet another fox cub appeared at this eyrie on a later visit, again, by its relative size, from the same den as the two first ones. It seemed that this pair of eagles had a taste for fox-flesh, a taste certainly not to human liking.

By early July the single eaglet was fully fledged and as usual looked fully capable of flying for all of a fortnight before it did fly.

On 14th July, however, the eyrie was bare of either occupant or prey, a tawdry, trampled-flat platform with the only life about it a few blue-bottle flies.

Prey at the 1961 eyrie consisted of grouse, rabbit, ptarmigan and fox cub. Decor used periodically by this pair was of rowan, heather, great woodrush, common rush, crowberry, dry green moss, grey lichen and, once, a sprig of juniper.

1962 was the first of the really bad eagle years, though this I did not suspect at the time. Pair 'A' had one sub-standard egg which on its eventual removal by myself (when it had become obvious, by late May, that it would not hatch) proved to be addled.

Pair 'B', back on a vulnerable eyrie site, again (as per the grape-vine) suffered the loss of the female. I paid a very early morning visit to the eyrie to confirm this to find the male eagle attempting to hatch the two eggs, an attempt he gave up; probably this was just as well for even if he had hatched them he could not have hunted for the necessary prey *and* given the necessary brooding, vital to the very young eaglets, as well.

Pair 'C' reared one young successfully, in my first year of studying this pair.

Pair 'D' also reared one eaglet, which proved, again unknown to me at the time, to be its last success to date (1971).

It was 8th July before I managed to visit the remote glen of Pair 'C', leaving home at 4.15 a.m. on my push-bike (a very apt description for the bike on the hilly road I had to travel). After spying the face of the 'eagle glen', leg-weary after the long walk from where I had left my bike, glad of any excuse for a rest, I finally located the eyrie in use, by the betraying evidence of breast feathers of previously plucked prey, clinging, light-coloured against its dark structure, to the outer edge of the eyrie. This was one of five sites which this particular pair have.

It was 8 a.m. before I drew near to the eyrie, and when within a few yards, I saw the head of a fully fledged eaglet turned to look at me. One look was apparently enough, for so rapidly that I still remember my incredulity, the eaglet walked to the outer edge of the eyrie and, flinging itself off, flew with every appearance of ease across the wide glen, to turn south up the passage of the burn in the glen bottom, and disappear from sight about half a mile up the glen. I was left with only the empty eyrie to compensate for my early morning travail. Remains of grouse were most in evidence and, beside these remains, a huge grey 'casting' lay, fully six inches long and an inch in diameter, the indigestible remains of a few meals, ejected by the eaglet, a habit common to birds of prey. Interesting as this was I was determined, having come so far, to make one last attempt to get at least one photograph of the eaglet, and hoping that its relative inexperience in flying might let me get within camera distance, I struck out in the direction of where the eaglet had vanished. After having played me such a scurvy trick at the eyrie, luck now relented, for I had no difficulty in spotting the grounded eaglet sitting in the long heather, near to the burn at the bottom of the glen. Upon seeing me it began flapping awkwardly with its wings, strutting comically downhill meantime, but quite unable to take off without the advantage of the elevation which the eyrie site had given it. The burn eventually halted its ungainly progress and I took as many photographs as I wanted before leaving it, both parents watchful high above, and commencing my long trudge homewards.

Prey seen on my one visit consisted of grouse, and decor was non-existent.

1963 proved to be just as bad in breeding success for 'my' eagles. Pair 'A' freshened up one eyrie but laid no egg. Pair 'B' reared one eaglet, as did Pair 'C', while Pair 'D' laid the first of a dismal succession of addled eggs.

Pair 'C' I visited at weekly intervals, distant as it was. Her clutch was two, and they both hatched though one 'chick' was very markedly smaller than the other. It eventually succumbed to slow starvation at about seven to eight weeks old after a long period of misty weather which must have made hunting for the parents very difficult. Had there been plenty of prey available I have no doubt whatever but that both young would have survived. This particular 1963 eyrie I have written of more fully in *Highland Deer Forest*. Suffice to say here that the surviving eaglet left the eyrie on 13th July and that it was on this occasion that I experienced the most persistent 'attacks' by an adult eagle, before or since.

Prey noted at this eyrie consisted of grouse, black water vole, bank vole, lamb, ring-ousel and red deer calf. Lamb I saw for the first time at any eyrie and it was present on only one occasion though the glen was 'full' of blackfaced sheep.

Decor was practically non-existent, a spray or two of rowan, a clod of grass, a little spray of crowberry and once, sphagnum moss.

1964 was even worse. From four pairs of eagles only one eaglet was reared successfully. Pair 'A' again did not nest, though the pair were definitely in the glen, Pair 'B' reared one from two hatched, Pair 'C' laid two eggs, which unaccountably vanished in April. This eyrie was accessible to fox and was also one which was known of by the estate stalker so that it could have been fox or human. Pair 'D' laid one egg which again was addled. The female incubated until late May before she gave up and I removed the egg for analysis.

Pair 'B' were back at the eyrie they used in 1960. I first visited it on 12th April. From below, as I approached, it looked freshly made up, and sure enough, when I cautiously craned over to look into it from above, there was the eagle incubating. She did not suspect my presence and I watched for some time. Once she raised herself off her clutch and, after rearranging the two eggs, turned completely round to sit now with her head into the cliff edge of the nest. On 25th April I visited the eyrie again, and again came in from above, undetected. I took a photograph of the incubating eagle and not even the 'clunk' of the focal plane shutter alerted her. I left her sitting as I had done on my first visit, quite unsuspicious. It would have been so easy to shoot her had I so desired. On 3rd May her eggs had hatched, and as she raised herself at one moment to change position I saw the chicks, about three to four days old. Watching from above there was a very definite difference in her 'sitting' position from that of the incubation period. When incubating she had had her wings tight to her body; today while brooding she had her wings held out slightly from her body, and every now and again she rose up slightly as if because of movement from her young. On 8th May the female took off from the eyrie's edge as I drew near. The young 'cheeped' incessantly as I took a photograph or two and then left. Remains of two grouse lay on the nest. One eaglet only was on the eyrie when I next went out to it; its nest mate had vanished. Again the remains of two grouse lay on the eyrie.

May 24th was a very misty day and I had difficulty in finding the eyrie. I disturbed a small herd of deer on my way out and watched them disappear, a ghostly file, breasting a nearby ridge. At the eyrie the eaglet was beginning to show signs of feathers, and traces of rabbit fur were caught on the nest structure. I sat back from the edge of the cliff above the eyrie to change the film in my camera and while doing so I heard the unmistakable 'swoosh' of eagle wings. Scarcely able to believe it, I crept across and peered over the edge. There below me on the eyrie was the female eagle, but to the obvious disappointment of the 'cheeping' eaglet, without prey. Watching, I saw her caress and gently preen the eaglet, incongruous as these words may seem as applied to a bird with which the adjective 'gentle' can rarely be justified. Ceasing this she picked up a large tuft of heather from the inner edge of the nest and rearranged it to her satisfaction on the outer edge. She then resumed her preening of the eaglet with that huge beak, more designed for tearing prey to pieces than this tender caressing of the young eaglet. As for the eaglet, like a young child having its grubby face and hands washed by its mother, it obviously could see no purpose in this, but wanted only food, of which there was none available.

This eaglet flew between 14th and 18th of July; my last visit, on the latter date, disclosed the usual tawdry, flattened platform of an 'end of the season' eyrie. Prey had been grouse, rabbit, lamb remains, and red deer calf.

1965 followed the same pattern. Pair 'A' again laid no eggs though the pair were resident. Pair 'B' reared one eaglet on their inaccessible (except to shooting) eyrie, so that all I could do was keep a watching brief from a high point over a mile away, which overlooked the eyrie. Pair 'C' laid two eggs but only hatched one, and here the hatched eaglet had vanished on my second visit, on 16th May. Pair 'D' laid two eggs but did not hatch either of them.

Of this pair I wrote on 20th May: 'Visited this eyrie today and to my surprise and very great pleasure the female flew from it as I arrived, her head glinting yellow-gold in the sunlight. I pressed on to the eyrie's edge, elated and expecting to find young eaglets at last in this glen. Elation went flat as a punctured balloon when I saw two unhatched eggs on the eyrie. One was addled, the other seemed to contain a chick, obviously dead, as this egg was ahering to the lining of the nest, probably through moisture seeping from it. With no hope whatever, but because I had to take advantage of every chance, no matter how remote, I left this egg and removed the other for analysis. On 30th May I returned to find the female had covered completely, with a layer of heather and an absolutely fresh spray of birch, the egg I had left. This egg I also removed for analysis.'

I visited Pair 'C' on 2nd May, leaving home at 4 a.m. The sky was just reddening to the east. A lark was singing and a thrush trying a few notes, while from a loch edge came the strident voices of awakening gulls. A rank of firs on a skyline ahead was etched, a black, toothed silhouette against the lightening sky. Coming past the house of my colleague, the stalker of that estate, I was amused as about a dozen stags jumped out of his garden while he blissfully slept. I hoped he had no spring cabbage planted, for he would certainly have none now. Farther on a small herd of deer were so avidly grazing that I was very close before they saw me, and they decamped hastily. A greenshank rose from the heathery flat almost on the very ridge top, about 2,500 ft high, with her incessant liquid whistle of alarm, and a pair of teal rose off a small lochan. Arriving at the face opposite the eyrie side of the glen I sat down to spy. The second eyrie was in use; I could see, with elation, an adult eagle, apparently, by her stooping and coming erect actions, feeding young. As I watched, weariness forgotten, she ceased this and settled down to brood her young. Descending the steep face of the glen I crossed the burn at the bottom and commenced the climb, legs aching again, up to the eyrie. As I did so, another adult eagle appeared and flew low over the eyrie, repeating this twice more, head bent down as if scrutinizing or communicating with the female still on it. I arrived, however, within twenty yards of the eyrie, its unseen occupant paying no heed to the 'warning' of its mate. Another few yards and she heard me as I stumbled on a heather-hidden rock and off she came to be joined by her mate, both of them 'dark-headed' eagles compared with the pale gold of others I had seen.

95

The eyrie held a young eaglet of only a few days, and an unhatched egg. Remains of three grouse lay at one edge. I left the unhatched egg until the following week and then removed it. My next visit was on May 16th, to find a repeat of the previous year, an empty eyrie. Fox or human agency? The latter seemed the more likely.

In late July I spied across at Pair 'B's' eyrie to see a well-developed eaglet doing wing exercises, half-hopping, half-flying, from one edge of the eyrie to the other, wings flapping energetically; it was obviously not going to be long before flying.

Prey on my two visits to the eyrie of 'C' had been grouse and black water vole.

1966 was disastrous. Pair 'A' laid no eggs; Pair 'B' laid no eggs; Pair 'C' laid no eggs (I heard of an eagle having been trapped in that area); Pair 'D' laid eggs as usual but, also as usual, did not hatch. I went there on May 14th and at first sight the signs were good: the eyrie was freshened up. I had my son Michael with me and I will never forget the utter disgust and disappointment on his face as he saw, on the eyrie we had walked so many miles to see, one unhatched egg and the scattered pieces of the shell of a second one, probably part eaten by the eagle herself, behaviour known to have occurred with peregrine falcons, a bird even more disastrously affected by the damnable effect of pesticides than the eagle.

After the depressing situation of 1966 it was more than heartening to find two pairs with young in 1967, Pairs 'B' and 'C' each of which reared one eaglet. Pair 'A' laid no eggs and Pair 'D' carried on with its dismal annual egg-laying and non-hatching sequence, laying one egg which, on 9th May, seemed addled, with a bad smell coming from it and a damp patch on the nest below it. The female was sitting, a very light-coloured bird with a head nearer white than golden. I left the egg though I knew in my heart it would not hatch and when I returned on 18th May it was gone. Pair 'B' were nesting on their inaccessible site again, and again I kept a long-distance vigil on it until the eaglet flew.

I was left then with Pair 'C' to make regular visits to. On 13th May I left at 4 a.m. accompanied by Michael, now almost as much of an 'eagleophile' as I was myself. The high summit ridge which we had to cross was quite clear as we began the steep slog up it, but before we reached the peat hags and innumerable small lochans of the narrow flat on top, mist, and really thick mist at that, was enshrouding it. Inevitably we got 'wandered' and for all of an anxious hour we probed here and there, retracing our steps more often than I care to remember. Eventually we struck off in the right direction and after we had descended a little way into the 'eagle' glen we suddenly entered 'another world' of bright sunshine. The female eagle flew above as we neared her eyrie, to be joined by her mate just as we reached it. Michael reached the nest first and the almost beatific smile which illumined his face was more than sufficient before his words, 'There's a chick.'

The eaglet was small but lively, cheeping incessantly, and three grouse lay near it. We left quickly after photographing eyrie and occupant.

On 18th June Michael took Barry Auld, a close friend, over to check on it. All was well and the prey they noted was very interesting, the remains of a young raven and of a common gull. Again *both* parents were seen.

June 24th saw the remains of a red deer calf as prey and a very young featherless ring-ousel which must have been actually taken from a nest; no doubt its nest mates had suffered a similar fate. On 1st July the prey was blue hare and on the 9th remains of a red deer calf. The eaglet had left the nest on 15th July but it was only about thirty yards away, perched beside a huge rock. It was very misty so that I was not seen until very near the eaglet, but one look was enough for it. A characteristic curtsy to space and it was off, to vanish in the mist.

Prey at the nest on our visits had been grouse, hare, gull, raven, ring-ousel nestling, black water vole and deer calf. Very little decor was seen apart from a spray or two of rowan.

In 1968 an eyrie of Pair 'A' had been freshened up but on a first look it appeared empty. As usual, I thought, and was about to go when I spotted an egg part hidden in the stalks to one side of the structure, not in the centre, which was in fact not hollowed out but flat-looking. The egg was quite cold and wet with rain. Deserted, but why? The egg was removed for analysis. Pair 'B' had at last chosen to use the eyrie at which I had built a hide in 1964. Pair 'C' had two eggs and hatched two chicks. Pair 'D' had not nested at all.

It was 11th May before I next visited Pair 'B' and was duly installed in the very cramped hide by Michael at 8 a.m. The female left as we approached; she had been brooding two chicks of about a week old. Three grouse and four black water vole lay on the nest.

Barely fifteen minutes after Michael had left the female landed on the nest with a terrific 'swoosh' of giant wings but left almost at once, to return moments later and settle down to brood her young. Every so often she was apparently heaved up by the chicks, though how chicks so small could cause the 'upheaval' of the adult eagle I cannot imagine. After an hour or so she left and was gone for half an hour, during which time the markedly larger chick spent most of the time in savagely pecking its nest mate, often about the head but at other times at whatever part of it was nearest. During her absence from the actual nest the female passed by several times, twice perching near to the nest, and each time she spent much of her time in balancing with her wings open in the strong northerly updraught. She came back on, and settled again for almost an hour, at one moment cocking her head to one side at hearing a shepherd's dog barking in the glen far below. I cannot describe what an immense thrill it was to watch an adult eagle, more often seen only as a black silhouette against the sky, at close range while she was quite relaxed, even though I had the uncomfortable feeling that her keen eyes were quite capable of penetrating the thin camouflage of my hide. On 19th May the smaller chick was gone, which hardly surprised me after what I had seen on the 11th.

I spent another uncomfortable but intensely interesting few hours on 2nd June. The chick was alone on the eyrie and it was 9 a.m. before the female came in, but with only a small sprig of rowan in her beak. She left at once and ten minutes later the cock arrived with a plucked grouse and, dropping it unceremoniously beside the eaglet, departed at once. The eaglet, obviously ravenous, tried to peck bits from the grouse but gave up at last and went to sleep, seemingly impervious to the fine drizzle of rain. It was after midday before the female came in and at once began to feed the eaglet, after which she allowed it to creep under her breast and sleep off its feed of fully half the grouse. This eaglet flew in the third week of July after giving me some of the most absorbing hours of eagle watching I have ever had. Pair 'C', incidentally, reared both chicks successfully.

Prey seen that year was grouse, rabbit, blue hare and black water vole. Very little decor was used on either eyrie.

1969 was a red-letter year for me (despite the bitter blow of knowing that I was to leave Culachy in July of that year), because my 'home' pair, Pair 'A', at last laid one egg, hatched it, and reared the eaglet successfully. Pair 'B' laid two eggs, as did Pair 'C' and Pair 'D'. This was the first time I had ever, in fourteen years, seen all four eyries with eggs, and I had enough daft optimism to believe they would all be successful. I should have known better. Pairs 'A' and 'B' reared successfully, one and two eaglets respectively, but Pair 'C' unaccountably, after rearing two in 1968, failed completely; only one addled egg of the two laid remaining on the eyrie on 24th May. Pair 'D' ran true to form and both eggs were addled.

Prey seen that year was grouse and ptarmigan. The decor was heather and juniper, bearberry and rowan.

Moving to Torridon meant the end of weekly visits to eyries now nearly a hundred miles away, but nevertheless I made as many visits as possible.

In 1970 Pair 'A', which I had hoped would now be breeding regularly, did not even lay an egg. Pair 'B' reared one young, Pair 'C' again reared two, and Pair 'D' again failed.

Prey seen on our limited visits was grouse (once a tiny chick) and fox (a well-grown cub).

In 1971 Pair 'A' again did not lay; Pair 'B' laid two eggs and reared two until the seven-week stage, when one vanished—the survivor flew safely. Pair 'C' did exactly the same as Pair 'B'. Pair 'D' laid two addled eggs, removed for analysis.

Prey noted was grouse and black water vole.

Since going to Torridon I have been able to check up on the eyries of a resident pair here. In 1969, 1970 and 1971 they reared one eaglet annually, though natural prey in this area seems even scarcer than at 'home', with the possible exception of ptarmigan and sea birds.

Some facts and figures on 'my' four pair of Monadhliaths eagles may be, indeed should be, interesting.

Eyrie 'A', which is adjacent to 'B' and 'C', has only reared four young since and including 1957, that is four in fifteen years. There are seven sites. In 1957 the female was shot on Site 1; in 1958 one eaglet was reared on Site 1; in 1959 the female reared one eaglet on Site 4; in 1960, believed killed; in 1961 one eaglet was reared on Site 7; in 1962 one substandard addled egg was laid on Site 1; 1963 to 1968 no eggs laid; 1969 one eaglet was reared on Site 3; 1970 and 1971 no eggs laid. From 1957 to 1971 I have never seen more than one egg laid on Eyrie 'A'.

Eyrie 'B', adjacent to 'A' and 'C', has reared thirteen young in fourteen years, including three sets of two, yet this is the eyrie which has suffered most persecution, the female being shot in three seasons, 1958, 1959 and 1962. There are three sites. In 1958 the female was shot on Site 1, in 1959 on Site 2, and in 1962 on Site 2. Two eaglets were reared on Site 3 in 1960 and on Site 1 in 1961. In 1963 she reared one on Site 1; in 1964 she reared one, from two eggs laid, on Site 3; in 1965 she reared one on Site 1; in 1966 there was no breeding, cause unknown; in 1967 she reared one on Site 1; in 1968 one from two eggs on Site 2; in 1969 two reared on Site 1; in 1970 one reared on Site 1 and in 1971 one reared from two eggs on Site 3.

Eyrie 'C', adjacent to 'A' and 'B', has reared eight eaglets in ten years, two sets of two included. There are five sites. In 1962 one eaglet was reared on Site 3; in 1963 one was reared from two eggs on Site 4; in 1964 two eggs on Site 1 vanished; in 1965 only one of the two eggs hatched on Site 3, chick vanished at fourteen days old. In 1966, no breeding, believed female trapped; in 1967 one was reared from one egg on Site 4; in 1968 two were reared on Site 1; in 1969 two eggs were laid, one was addled and one disappeared, on Site 4; in 1970 two were reared on Site 2; in 1971 two were hatched, one reared on Site 2.

Eyrie 'D', adjacent to 'C', has reared three only in thirteen years. There are now only three sites; there were four prior to 1963. In 1959 one eaglet was reared on Site 4; in 1960 one was reared on Site 3, one egg laid; in 1961 the female was shot on Site 1; in 1962 one eaglet was reared on Site 2; in 1963 no breeding; in 1964 one addled egg on Site 2; in 1965 two addled eggs on Site 2; in 1966 one addled egg, one eaten, on Site 3; in 1967 one addled egg on Site 2; in 1968 no breeding; in 1969 two addled eggs on Site 2; in 1970 no breeding and in 1971 two addled eggs on Site 2.

Eyrie 'A', then, reared four birds in fifteen years; 'B' thirteen in fourteen years; 'C' eight in ten years; 'D' three in thirteen years. The total of years of all four pairs was fifty-two. The total of young reared was twenty-eight, of which there were five pairs reared (ten birds), and eighteen singles. All the eggs which I sent for analysis had traces of pesticides.

9

Wild Highlands

THE Highlands of Scotland form the largest 'wild' area left to us in urbanized Britain today, offering scenery as fine as anywhere in the world and affording sanctuary to species of wildlife to which the presence of man is anathema. This very wilderness, at times to the point of near sterility, the relative lack of access roads and the type of weather which Highlanders have sometimes to endure rather than to enjoy, are all factors which I believe have preserved for all of us a part of Britain where it is still possible, even in these days of expanding population and urbanization, for man to get away from his fellow man, for at least his annual holiday, so that he can return, refreshed in mind and body, to the iron maw of industrialization and to the rubbing of shoulders, sometimes literally, with his fellows.

Attractive as this wild remoteness is to the urban visitor it is rarely as attractive to the local who may, familiarity breeding contempt, regard red deer as pests which compete with his sheep for the scant hill grazing, see the golden eagle with jaundiced eyes because one may occasionally take a lamb, and consider the wildcat and pine marten as animals to be killed whenever possible because they may *sometimes* cause havoc in an insecurely fastened henhouse. While writing of this last, I cannot resist telling the true story of a crofter who had great difficulty in getting his hens to go into his henhouse one night. Exasperated almost beyond endurance he at last got them 'herded' in with the aid of his well-trained collie, and shut them securely in. Next morning he found that *all* his hens were dead, while crouched in the most remote recess of his henhouse was a wildcat, also securely shut in the previous night.

There are definite drawbacks, mind you, to living in the Highlands. Few of the visitors who rhapsodize about their fortnight's holiday would last much longer than that, particularly in winter, when they discover the extremely high cost of even the very staples of life such as milk, meat and bread, the lack of chip shops, picture houses and pubs, the remoteness of secondary schools, hospitals and dentists, and the sheer savagery of the weather by no means uncommon in a Highland winter. Having said all this I would live nowhere else, but the very fact of the continuing drift away from the remoter areas of the Highlands of our young folk emphasizes very forcibly that those residents who feel as I do are very much a minority. Another factor, that many, very many, of the houses in our remoter areas in the north-west Highlands are being bought up by southerners (who can afford to offer *very* much higher prices than any local, so that they can use them primarily for 'holiday homes' while already having a house in the south to which they retire in winter) is no help, to put it mildly, in averting the continued drain of our local populations. Wiser heads than mine seem unable to solve this problem; I can only deplore it.

To me, however, the 'advantages' of urban life are far outweighed by the scenic beauty (even if, as the Skye crofter said, 'Scenery won't feed a cow') which surrounds me, and more particularly in the interest of the wildlife amid this scenery. But then man is essentially a gregarious animal while I am of that minority for whom solitude is not only endurable but enjoyable, and for whom encounters with wildlife have engrossing interest, even after more than twenty years of this.

Where else but in the 'wild Highlands' could one encounter, as I did, on an exceptionally lucky day once in all these years, red deer, roe deer, wildcat, fox and badger? Or watch an eagle caress its recently hatched 2 oz. down-clad chick with that impressive hooked beak, rarely used caressingly, to say the least? Where else can one sit, enthralled, above a rock slit, the den of a pair of pine martens, and listen to them 'chatter' inside its security? Or lie motionless and spellbound on the shingled beach of a sea-loch, its stoniness and dampness disregarded, while watching an otter swim nearer and nearer, alternately diving, leaving a chain of silvery bubbles, and surfacing, until it finally emerges among the golden-yellow seaweed, to go to sleep, curled up on a seaweed-covered boulder, not twenty yards from me? Where else, too, can one suddenly see, while ridge-walking at over 2,000 feet, a grey-speckled 'rock' suddenly become animated among its fellows and reveal itself as a ptarmigan, a scant few feet away, and, while trying to photograph this, have another scuttle secretively away, literally from one's very feet? Or, in winter, see, by a grey rock jutting from a snowdrift, a hen ptarmigan, whiter than the very snow, revealed only by the gleam of a beady black eye?

England has its relatively small number of wild red deer, but not amid the sometimes awesome savagery of rock and hill which makes the spectacle of the Highland red deer rut so utterly absorbing to me. The roaring and bluster of the stags echoing from the rock-strewn slopes of glen or coire, the sight of stags possessed by such a demon of unrest that they must vent their spleen on inoffensive tufts of heather or rushes (in doing so at times acquiring a chaplet of vegetation), and, most enthralling of all, the occasional sight of a battle between two aspirants for the overlordship of a group of hinds, who, in marked contrast, may be lying placidly chewing the cud—where but in the 'wild Highlands' can one see this without masking undergrowth or woodland to obscure your view?

Interesting indeed as I find all species of wildlife in the Highlands, red deer are my 'first love', closely followed by roe deer. To me red deer are also the most impressive of our animals, while roe are the most beautiful. There are still 'secrets' in both red and roe, as far as their natural history is concerned, to intrigue the naturalist, whether amateur or scientifically trained. An example common to both red and roe is in the annual casting of their antlers and their subsequent regrowth, whereas sheep, cattle and goats retain their 'headgear' for life. I am convinced that the antlers of deer (and antler is the correct terminology for the headgear of deer, not horns as correctly applied to that of sheep, goats and cattle) were originally for purposes of defence, even more than as fighting weapons in the relatively short mating season, and yet there are two major puzzles still to find convincing answers to. One of these is, why does the female of the species not carry antlers if they were primarily de-fensive weapons, and the second is, why are the males left defenceless for a considerable period each year, while their antlers are cast and growing anew? It is a romantic but unfortunately (for the sentimental) false idea that the stag is the leader and the defender of the hinds and their offspring, which means that the females themselves must defend, and do defend, their young until such time as they are able to rely on swiftness of foot as a primary defence in attack by predators.

Puzzling as this is today, when our major predators in the Highlands are fox and eagle (instead of wolf, bear and lynx), capable only of killing young deer (and even this does not occur sufficiently often to have real significance on our deer populations) it is even more puzzling to think that the same state of affairs was true of the days when wolf, bear, and lynx *were* predators on adult and juvenile deer alike. Left without defensive headgear, the mothers of both red deer calves and roe deer fawns, when motivated by maternal feelings, use their lashing forelegs tipped with hard black hooves to defend their young against fox or eagle, the dauntless courage of maternity ensuring that the very 'last ditch' desperation of this defence is normally sufficient against fox or eagle. One doubts whether this would have been sufficient when the now extinct larger predators still existed in Britain.

Male deer are, and were, left defenceless for a period of at least three months while the growth of new antlers replaces those cast by them. At this vulnerable period of their annual cycle male deer will also use lashing forelegs when, say, squabbling amongst themselves, and no doubt also in defence. Incapable as they seem to be of any deep affection towards the females they mate with or the young subsequently produced, male deer are motivated only to defend themselves and in the lack of predators on adult deer nowadays their antlerless state for a period each year signifies little. It must, one feels, have mattered very much more at one time, and so the puzzle remains. Why *do* deer cast their antlers? Why have females none?

Another intriguing and well-recognized habit of red deer in the Highlands is that of chewing strange objects, including cast antlers, bones of long-dead animals or birds, pieces of fabric, wood, and alloy (as left by the few occurrences of crashed 'planes throughout the Highlands) and, even more intriguing, the reliable occasional instance reported of the chewing of the 'fresh' carcase of small animal or bird, such as I had seen my 'tame' hind Beauty do (see Chapter 3). Deer have been seen on the Island of Rhum (a National Nature Reserve) chewing the carcases of Manx shearwaters: evidence, in some cases, pointing very strongly to the supposition that these birds had been killed by the deer and *not* picked up dead. Manx shearwaters nest in burrows, high up near the summit of Hallival,

The otter emerges onto a seaweed-covered rock.

A badger on rocky ground.

Ptarmigan in 'summer dress', a striking contrast to the snow-white winter plumage (below).

XLII

A very fine red deer stag in full velvet, late July.

A red deer stag in hard antler, late autumn.

XLIV

Deer sleep curled up like a dog, but only when they feel absolutely
secure.

Why *do* red deer stags have to lose and then regrow their antlers annually?

Bereft of their antlers, stags will rear up and lash out at each other with their hooves, just as the antlerless hinds do.

XLV

The first definite recording of twins born to a British red deer hind, on the island of Rhum.

A fine roe buck, one of our most attractive wild animals.

The antlered roe doe, a unique head in British roe history.

XLVIII

on Rhum, and so could be killed by a waiting red deer as they emerge from a burrow, before they could take wing. Apart from my personal experience with Beauty, which led me to believe *she* had, on occasion, killed birds trapped in netted strawberry beds, I have also personal knowledge of an enclosed red deer stag killing with his forelegs two cock pheasants at different times (the assumption being that they had 'lain tight' in long grass until it was too late), and then had chewed their feet completely off before leaving their carcases lying. This chewing habit, puzzling at first as it is, has been attributed, quite logically, to the very definite deficiency of calcium and phosphates in the largely acid, peaty soil of much of the Highlands and a consequent craving for bones etc. in Highland red deer.

It was from the island of Rhum, too, that in 1970 the first recorded eye-witness account of twins being born to a red deer hind came. The occurrence of twins in red deer is very, very rare and while I have personally seen, on two occasions only, a red deer hind with two very young calves, and know of reliable stalkers who have also seen this, we could never prove, though fairly certain ourselves, that they *were* cases of twins because we had not seen them being born. This left the possibility that the hind seen had 'adopted' an orphaned calf, a possibility which was accepted as being more likely than that she had borne twins. Knowing of the difficulty experienced with sheep in getting them to accept a 'strange' lamb in place of their own dead one (the usual procedure is to use the skin of the dead lamb as a 'coat' for the strange lamb so that the sheep would recognize it by scent), and also having personally witnessed, many times, the actual savagery with which red deer hinds have repulsed a tiny calf not their own, a tiny calf the very personification of attractiveness to our eyes, I believe personally that in the very few cases where two calves have been seen following a hind, that it is just as likely to have been twins as for one to have been 'adopted'. Be that as it may, the names of the two research workers, Fiona Guinness and John Fletcher, who actually witnessed the birth of both calves, a male and a female of 13 lb. 12 oz. each, will go down to posterity in the annals of red deer natural history. The hind which gave birth to the twins was one of a small group of hinds enclosed for research purposes, living in a very large enclosure under conditions comparable to natural habitat, if without the extensive range of our wild red deer. The father of the twins was a hummel stag, also in the enclosure for purposes of research. In deer circles there has been, in the past, controversy as

to whether a hummel (an antlerless stag) is capable of siring a calf.
I personally never doubted a hummel's potency and, in the case of
the Rhum twins, the potency and ability of the hummel could hardly
have been better demonstrated. I was lucky enough to be able to
see and photograph the twins while on a visit to Rhum some months
after their birth.

Witnessing the actual birth of a red deer calf 'in the wild' in the
Highlands is a comparatively rare experience which I have been
lucky to have had only once at sufficiently close quarters to be able
to see it well. Rare as this is, the witnessing of the birth of young to
a roe doe must be even more rare, in a species so much smaller than
red deer and one so adept in utilizing the cover of woodland undergrowth as roe deer are. A friend of mine, Alec MacKenzie, must
therefore be accounted very lucky in witnessing this while on a
'drive' through coniferous woodland for a fox which was killing
lambs in the area. Alec was one of the men posted at intervals
throughout the wood in places where there was a likelihood of seeing
and shooting any fox put forward by the numerous beaters employed
in 'driving' the wood. He was sitting absolutely still in sufficient
concealment to avoid being seen by a fox when he noticed a roe
deer in a small clearing fairly close to him. Within moments of his
first sight of her he saw her give birth to a fawn which she immediately began licking and cleaning. While still so engaged, only
minutes later and quite effortlessly, she gave birth to a second fawn,
which she also 'licked clean' before lying down with them both,
'taking cover' so well that even the concealed watcher could barely
see them. Some time elapsed before the beaters came through past
his position without his having seen any sign of fox. A shepherd's
collie was first to go by, within yards of the doe, frozen motionless
where she lay, without detecting her. Only moments later the dog's
owner came by, even nearer to the motionless doe, still trusting
everything to her utter immobility. Her trust was vindicated when
the collie's owner passed, as unsuspectingly as his dog had done.

In both red deer and roe deer, antlers, as most people will know,
are grown usually only by the male. Occurrences of antler growth
in roe does are, however, while still relatively rare and therefore
noteworthy, much more common than in red deer hinds. Where
antler growth does occur in a roe doe it is usually rudimentary—
perhaps only a spike of an inch or two in length on each side—and
almost invariably this is encased in 'permanent velvet', as in a buck

106

growing his annual 'new' antlers. An acquaintance of mine from Banffshire therefore shook me to the core when he telephoned me, in late May 1971, and told me that he had a dead roe doe to show me, which had a twelve-point antlered head. Now a normal head for a roe buck is one of six points and the only definite record I know of a twelve-point buck in Scotland was from the latter half of the last century, so that a twelve-point *buck*, even, was something to marvel at. But a twelve-point doe; it seemed too incredible for words. Knowing of my interest in wildlife my Banffshire friend put me forever in his debt by inviting me along to see and if necessary verify his own 'findings' in the matter. I could tell by his voice, even over the 'phone, that he could hardly believe the evidence of his own eyes, and he was a man with years of experience with roe deer.

I was still incredulous, quite frankly, when I arrived to see the dead roe. All doubt vanished when I was shown it, though my state of almost incredulous wonderment remained even as I satisfied myself and my friend that it *was* a doe, a doe with antlers more massive, well-pearled and with more points than by far the vast majority of bucks. In fact, though my friend had only 'claimed' twelve points for his doe she had, in *my* opinion, thirteen, having a point of an inch in length growing from the coronet at the base of the right antler, besides six definite ones on each antler. I cannot truthfully say it was a beautiful head but it was, and is, a head unique in British roe history, possibly unique even in Europe. Apart from the antlers, which were hard and clean of velvet, there were present on the roe *all* the normal outward attributes of a doe, even to the anal bush of stiff hair which *only* the doe grows and which can be likened to a small, shaving-brush-like tail. Examining her closely we detected two very small gonads, tight under the skin and invisible to the eye. She had no penis or penis sheath, nor had she an udder, though she had small teats. In my opinion she was seven to eight years old and had never had young in her life. Another 'first' which ensures for its owner a place in deer literature as long as this endures.

Index

Index

112